ANGELA RODAWAY was born in Winnipeg, Canada in 1918, but came to England when she was very small. Her parents rented two rooms in north London on the first floor of 10 Arundel Square. Before the end of her first school days they had moved to four ground floor and basement rooms in nearby Ellington Street, where her twin sisters were born in 1928. It is this Islington world of the twenties and thirties which she so wonderfully evokes in *A London Childhood*. Later the family had a house and café in Fore Street, Edmonton, but the café, owned by a benefactor, failed financially during the Depression. They then moved to Battersea in South London. During these years, Angela Rodaway took a number of jobs, mostly clerical, writing in between for magazines and studying theatre. She left home before she was eighteen, and the loss of her own home twice through wartime bombing 'weakened her liking for material possessions'.

At the war's end she was alone with a small son. For the next thirteen years she taught school in London, Derbyshire, Devonshire, Gloucestershire and Bristol, and in 1960 *A London Childhood* was published. In recent years she has worked with young Afro-Caribbean people, teaching drama. Angela Rodaway regards herself as a survivor, and has started writing again after many years. She lives in Bristol.

# A LONDON CHILDHOOD

*Angela Rodaway*

With a New Introduction
by the Author

Virago

# TO
# MY SISTERS

Published by VIRAGO PRESS Limited 1985
41 William IV Street, London WC2N 4DB

This edition offset from the first edition of the book,
published in 1960 by B.T. Batsford Ltd, London

Copyright © Angela Rodaway 1960
New introduction © by Angela Rodaway 1985

*British Library Cataloguing in Publication Data*
Rodaway, Angela
   A London childhood.
   1. Islington (London, England)——Social
   life and customs     2. London (England)——
   Social life and customs——20th century
   I. Title
   942.1′43083′0924        DA685.I8

   ISBN 0-86068-640-X

Printed in Finland by Werner Söderström Oy,
a member of Finnprint

# CONTENTS

# INTRODUCTION

In 1974, having been asked to give away prizes at Barnsbury Park School, I went back to North London to the area of Islington which I had known as a child. I reached the locality much too early and spent some time exploring the past.

The market was still there. It was now called "Chapel Market" although I had known it as Chapel Street. I was glad that it still existed since the Cattle Market in the Caledonian Road had gone and I had wondered how people had managed when no longer able to go "down the Cally".

As a child it had seemed so far, the trek down the Liverpool Road to the beginning of Ellington Street and the Church Gardens on the other side of the road. Now it was a stone's throw however much the memories of Offord Street and Furlong Road might cause me to linger. I crossed to the gardens and was dismayed a little at the forbidding height of the railings surrounding it and at the oppressive style of the church itself. Long ago it had not seemed like that. Perhaps children are used to things towering above them and do not much notice greater or lesser heights. The railings were too high to climb over and we saw only the gardens, especially the part to the south. In those days, there were bright green lawns and flower beds of scarlet geraniums, red hot pokers and bleeding hearts. To us these colours were perfect and the little borders of lobelia and alyssum with touches of bright golden yellow an unnecessary indulgence. Now the gardens seemed dingy and poor and overwhelmed by the railings and the church itself.

I crossed the Liverpool Road again, not to Ellington Street where I had lived, but to Bride Street. I had never walked along it in all the years we had lived in the area. We did not connect it with a bride and I cannot think how it had come to be named unless in a spirit of derision. Now people spoke of it in just the tones that they had used in the past, but the smells were different, somehow updated, for the smoke from marijuana hung in the air. There were small shops still at the Westbourne Road end, and, across the road the huge and severe angles of St Clement's church.

Ellington Street looked wider than I remembered, perhaps because I had expected it to seem shrunken and had overcompensated. Mr Moore, the chemist, had kept his shop on the corner and his fascinating array of bottles and perfumed soaps had lent an air of refinement to the street. He would give me a present of soap at Christmas. A number of shopkeepers gave gifts at that season but I have no doubt that such gracious habits have long since been relinquished. The shop had been restructured and was now a "mini-market".

I had known every crack in the pavement down Ellington Street, a memory reinforced by numerous small scars, but the cracks and the puddles were no longer there, for the paving stones, worn, as they had been in concentric circles like ripples, had been replaced by slabs of a synthetic evenness. The little houses at the Liverpool Road end of the street were still there. We had once envied the people who lived in them because, with their small wooden gates and front gardens, they had seemed to us like cottages that we learned of in fairy tales, and so had an air of romance.

Arundel Square I had left until last although my first memories were of there. The houses were the same, although no allotments adorned the railway embankment, but the rank grass of the square itself, and the tennis courts had been replaced by concrete, the unsympathetic surface of which was furnished with play equipment for children. I remembered its exclusiveness, the large key that we so proudly held and the people from the vicarage in their tennis whites on summer evenings.

It was with a shock that I remembered why I had come and I realised that I was in danger of being late. I began to run, recollecting, as I did so, that I was taking the same route that I had run half a century ago and was still in danger of being late for school.

When I reached Barnsbury Park the feeling was confirmed of being back in another time, for, as I entered the grimed brick school building, the same smells struck me, of cedar wood pencils and something else, perhaps unsalubrious but welcome to me who still like the odour of shabby wet clothes and find the smell of the London underground the most exciting in the world.

There were changes nevertheless. The children, as we passed through the hall, looked much the same, only neater and cleaner than we had been, but it was murmured to me that the incidence of overcrowding in the area was still the highest in the United Kingdom, and that included the Gorbals of Glasgow, and that now seventy-five per cent of the school's pupils had not been born in Great Britain. This became obvious as the children walked up for their prizes and I shook each dry little hand.

The school had been extended and had taken in what had been the Central School, in fact this was now the main part of the school, being bigger and better-equipped. ROSLA (the Raising of the School Leaving Age) had also had its effect, the school-leaving age being now sixteen instead of fourteen, and there was an active Pupil-Parent-Teachers Association. It was two of these young members of the Association who acted as hostesses during the fête after the prize-giving. There were stalls and side-shows set out in the playground and a degree of organisation and co-operation that I cannot help feeling would have been far beyond the capabilities of people in my day.

We went inside to watch pupils perform and I was reminded of what this had meant ten school-generations ago. There was a country dance called "Gathering Peasecods". It was taught always in the same class and I suspect that that teacher knew no other dance, for year after year successive "Class sixes" gathered peasecods, learning to do it, at first, without music, under the playground shed that was without walls, like a Dutch barn, and the girls stumbled through "set and turn single" – like cream that has been thinned – and caused chaos by forgetting which was the left hand and which the right.

As a consequence, when I was told in this later decade that some of the girls would dance for us, I expected something similar and even wondered if "Gathering Peasecods" would feature. Instead there was a row of girls looking self-composed and serious in their concentration. Music started and they began a "line dance" that I had seen rows of young people performing at "discos". They moved with a kind of strict precision that young people achieve only when self-directed and working with their peers, and it was obvious who was "boss" and who would "get it", subsequently, for placing a foot late by a split second.

My second school, which was Highbury Hill High School for Girls, I had passed a number of times during the seventies and could not really believe that much had changed in one decade. I knew I was wrong, as soon as I approached, for a very new, very bright red brick building occupied the space next to the main school. This was the new science wing.

By 1984 Highbury Hill High School had become Highbury Fields School for Girls. I went into the main entrance, which we never did, but all other ways seemed barred. Vaguely conscious of the portrait photograph on my right, of a woman of somewhat Victorian aspect, I faced an even larger portrait of a man of African origin. This was new. I asked who it was and was told that two other schools had amalgamated with Highbury and this was the head of one of them. And the one on the right? I looked again. Yes, the face was familiar but younger than we had known it. This was Miss Kyle, "Kylo" as we called her, tall, broad, majestic, with a long, pale face and high forehead, black-gowned and with black hair, centre-parted and drawn back severely into a luxuriant bun. The proximity of the two portraits seemed incongruous to me. Then I knew that to Kylo my misgivings would have been naïve and even vulgar. She would calmly and academically have discussed with him the joy and difficulties of running a school for girls, and I knew too what would have been her attitude regarding some of the "problems" that beset our schools today, that if any of our girls had needed, on religious grounds, to wear trousers or yashmaks or head-ties (in addition to the school uniform, of course) she would have accepted it without question or comment, except to introduce Comparative Religion into assembly and to point out to other pupils that intelligent people understood these things and did not remark on them. She would not have used the word "cool" in the way that we do today but she would certainly have appreciated its meaning.

The school had been founded by two maiden ladies. It was selective, both as regards the attainment of would-be pupils and the ability of parents to pay fees. By 1929, when I began there, something of the original attitude remained. With the exception of the stout and rubicund hall porter, we were all maiden ladies and the emphasis was on scholastic achievement, although it was conceded on occasion that marriage also was a career, and by now a number of state scholarships were being granted, otherwise I should never have gone there.

The feeling had changed. There had always been a kind of intensity about school, an intensity that had to do only with ourselves, with older girls, with the mistresses who taught us, and with academic attainment. Perhaps this was because there was so little else in our lives, although we regarded ourselves as knowledgeable and sophisticated since, for some of us, Virginia Woolf and others of the set then flourishing in Bloomsbury, were our heroes and their heterosexual and homosexual couplings common knowledge. Now there were men around in the school, two male teachers and others waiting about in the reception hall. The head was a married woman. All the furniture was different. Instead of the wooden desks, the lids of which we used to bang shut, there were those ubiquitous iron-legged, stacking tables and chairs that the more discerning nowadays call "arse trays". They were fire-proof, which commended them to the authorities, but the sound they made as they were moved over floors and the difference they made to the acoustics of the whole building were anathema to me. When they were stacked a room would seem empty as it never had been in our day.

In the hall there was preserved, on the platform, the great, carved oak chair, like a throne, in which Kylo had sat for her photograph. It looked like something in a museum. The benches had gone – people could not remember them – solid benches of creamy limed oak which were later, after Kylo's retirement and long after my day, stained a warm mahogany. The impressive gallery had gone too, having been walled in and used as an extra room. Space was obviously at a premium, and spaciousness. We had been used to hiding in the library which had bookshelves jutting out from the walls to make little niches in which one could sit and bury oneself in a book. The present library was bright and open. One could not bury anything in it let alone oneself. I felt that, if anything had gone it was a certain solidity and graciousness. Perhaps it had gone, not only from here, but from everywhere that I had known. Then I stood thankfully in the gym. It was quite unchanged. All the apparatus was the same and even that which was moveable was still kept in the same places.

But some of the railings had gone from Highbury Fields, I thought jealously. Sheep had once grazed there sometimes, presumably destined for the cattle market in the Caledonian Road. Today the place seems totally unsympathetic to sheep. I went down through Fieldway Crescent and past the public library where, for so many years, I had worshipped silently but freely. Looking towards the other side of the Holloway Road I could see that all the grand, overbearing railings had gone from around the church gardens opposite, and wire netting stretched between the old and blackened brick pillars. Around the graves and the flower beds were fences of wooden stakes strung together on twisted wire. For the first time I looked at the name of the church, St Mary Magdalene with St James Holloway. There were winter-pruned rose bushes where the geraniums had been.

As soon as I looked across Liverpool Road I knew that "Bride Street revisited" would be an anti-climax. Very new brick buildings graced the other side of the road and stretched away east towards Westbourne Road. Bride Street, notorious for many decades, had become part of a modern housing estate. At the other end, on the corner, was the familiar pub and the sweet shop next to it was still there and still under the same name. St Clement's church was hollow-eyed, a ruin. It would not remain standing for much longer.

The backs of the Bride Street houses had held almost the

same degree of dreadful fascination as had the street, although not quite of the same kind, and these back yards had given on to the long, beaten earth "gardens" of Ellington Street. There would be no more raucous singing before the church bells began on lazy sluttish Sunday mornings, no more of the screaming fights that caused the inhabitants of the other houses to hang out of their windows to try to peer through the murky glass opposite and there would be no more clucking of hens in the daytime and no more crowing of cocks in the small hours. It was this last and the singing that evoked in me the most poignant feelings and memories.

Ellington Street was being improved, but only in parts, as yet. Now, at regular intervals, one of the new synthetic paving stones had been removed and a tree planted in the earth. Houses were for sale. Some had obviously already been bought and modernised. The architecture had taken on a new significance. All but one had suffered some changes and that one stood defiantly amongst the rest, black with the grime of half a century and with rags at the windows.

I had gone a long way since the Ellington Street days, but Ellington Street had come a long way too, for Ellington Street was looking up, now that it no longer looked down on Bride Street and I wondered if I need have "gone" anywhere at all.

On to Arundel Square along the east side where we had lived and where the rows of bell pushes now proclaimed that the houses had been divided into self-contained flats. The north side, with its imposing stuccoed pillars and porticos, had been painted a stark, glossy white, cold in the winter afternoon. On a warm day the severity of the whiteness might seem less violent. The gloss was wholly regrettable. The stucco and the plaster were meant to imitate stone. When they were treated with this in mind, the result could be elegant.

I went through the open gate into the square that had become a concrete recreation ground. There was still a small patch of grass on the west side and a dark brown, small pre-fabricated building in the middle that seemed to be used for community activities. Over the crisp, frosty grass to the railings by the railway line. It was still there but looked derelict. A goods train grumbled through slowly showing that, at least, the line was not abandoned, but either side of it were tips of rubbish, tins, bottles and bits of plastic. The rag and bone man, with his cry of "Rags, bottles and bones!", pronounced, as nearly as possible, as one syllable, obviously had ceased to ply his trade. The allotments had gone. The slopes of the railway embankments were no longer cultivated, nor cared for in any way. Where allotments had been was only a small wilderness of old brambles and dead grass. I was reminded of "Elegy in a Country Churchyard". Evidence of accumulated wealth was all around but a certain spirit had decayed. The shade and the shrubs and the secret hiding places had gone. The square had the atmosphere of an open-plan office. It was reminiscent of the change that had come over the school library.

There was a path running diagonally from the gate to another gate that gave onto Westbourne Road. Schoolgirls were walking happily along it, using it as a short cut. They conversed in accents that had nothing of the careful cultivation to which ours had been subject and they used words which, half a century ago, would never have crossed my lips, although they do now, on occasion. Then I reflected that these were young people who, if they had got to Highbury at all in the old days, by way of the eleven plus, would, on reaching a fourteenth birthday, simply have disappeared from there, unnoticed, unsung and having achieved nothing.

East, past Barnsbury Park School that belonged to an even earlier time, for me. Left along Liverpool Road and down Station Road. It was "Highbury Station Road" now but we never called it that. Why should we have specified "Highbury" when there wasn't anywhere else? We had gone to Highbury Fields that way on Sunday mornings with my father. My brother and I shared a push chair, taking turns to ride in the strange contraption, made of wood and fashioned like a deck chair but with a strip of carpet instead of canvas. My brother rode first because he was younger and I was accorded the privilege of walking through streets where we were known. For some reason, on one occasion, my father decided that I must ride first and I screamed all the way down this road at the indignity of my position.

Now I was making for Highbury Corner, for the Underground station on the new Victoria Line. I was only eight minutes from Oxford Circus which was a world away.

I was reluctant to leave and went into a café, carrying my coffee cup to the only table that had a vacant place. Two girls were sitting there. In my day an elderly woman who sat at our table in a public place would have been politely ignored. We learned to put a psychological wall around ourselves, a wall that denied the existence of anything outside it, the size of the barrier being exactly adapted to the amount of space required. (I learnt this later as part of "Method" acting.) I still do it. I did it now. But the girls looked up, smiling and one of them said "Hi!" and then resumed their conversation. They spoke in the same way as the girls in the square, and I suddenly loved their London voices and wished that they had not needed to leave before I was able to insinuate myself into a gap in the chatter. My own design for living and that of my contemporaries seemed good to me and many of the good things had gone, but I had an immediate conviction that some aspects of the "open plan" might be better, much better.

*Angela Rodaway, Bristol, 1984*

# PREFACE

One of the chapters in this book was originally given in an altered form as a radio talk, and I should like to make appropriate acknowledgment to the British Broadcasting Corporation for its reproduction here.

.        .        .

Reminiscence, however grim the events remembered, is nearly always nostalgic. I have not minimised the grimness—although, in retrospect, some of it is funny.

Things have changed appreciably, but not completely and one has misgivings. These began twenty-five years ago at about the time that the story in this book ends. They began when I realised that, in a comparatively prosperous community, the individual who remained poor, either through unavoidable circumstances or from choice, for his own individual ends, could no longer buy "two penn'orth of pot-herbs". In twenty-five years we have progressed considerably along this road for now he cannot even find anywhere to live.

A. R.

*Spring, 1960*

# CHAPTER I

## *LESS HUMBLE BEGINNINGS*

I W A S seven years old in the year nineteen twenty-five and many things were different, then, from what they are now. Perhaps rich people were richer. Certainly the very poor were in greater numbers, and it was to the latter class that we belonged. We were never so ill-dressed that toes came bare through our broken shoes, but rarely were we so well shod that the naked soles of our feet did not touch the pavements as we walked.

Time is a dull line to string events on. Things count for more or less according to the thread that runs through them. Perhaps, though, the first memory is of first importance, in that it is supposed to indicate one's "life style", one's key attitude to life, the essential situation which, in personal relationships, one constantly recreates. Mine puts me in a bad light straight away.

It is round about the time of my second birthday and there are the wooden bars of a cot, which had been made by my father. I am outside the cot, not in it. Through the bars and just on a level with my face is the head of a baby, with startled blue eyes, and his milk-white face is pursed voluptuously round the teat of his feeding-bottle. It is easy to take the bottle, through the bars, climb on to the prickly, dark green sofa, surrender to two minutes' utter bliss, then put the bottle back again, empty. The baby does not even cry. His face wears a look of hurt astonishment.

Later I adopted a maternal attitude towards this younger brother and used to "mind" him, if we were left alone in the room. He had a soft, pale, pliant face and sometimes I would pull it about, stretching down his eyelids, pushing up his nose or pulling back his cheeks so that his mouth went wide, quite gently, not to hurt him, merely to make him look ugly, so that I could call our mother to look. On baking day, I made a "baby" of my own and the dough felt just like my brother. When it was cooked it was not the same at all.

My father had iron-grey hair, short, curly and resilient, like a spade beard upside-down. His face was mahogany, his neck raw beef and his eyes were the washed blue of shadows on snow. He loved wild life and had lived in Canada for a long time. It was there that, one evening, his pet bull-dog had gone wild, leapt at him and clung to his upper lip, until the flesh tore. My father had sat all night in a hut, holding the edges of the wound together. It healed with a wide scar, nevertheless, and, to cover it, he grew a moustache which he never shaved off. The bull-dog died, years later, after fighting with a badger, and it was my father's pride that the badger, too, was mortally wounded.

My father's eyes, apart from their colour, always seemed remarkable to me. The folds about them were so deep that the eyes seemed almost to be double-lidded, like those of some reptiles and birds. The lashes were sparse and white. They had not become so but had remained like that, for he had been white-headed as a boy and nicknamed "Snowball". He had been bandy too, and, although he was so no longer, yet his gait, whether he walked or ran, had something eccentric about it, characteristic of people who have been bow-legged.

Even when very young I was quite familiar with the word "bandy", and I think there must have been many more people afflicted with bow-leggedness then.

I had ample opportunity to examine my father's face, because he used to take my brother and me, one on each knee, and tell us stories. These kept us quiet and out of the way so that my mother could get on with things that were more important. The stories were, of course, "a lot of nonsense", and it is only in recent years that I have realised how good the nonsense was, how fluent the inventiveness and how rare the gift. Then, we took it for granted; it was a valueless indulgence like cheap sweets and paper chains at Christmas. The stories were always moral, but not obtrusively so, or we would laugh and refuse to accept anything so obviously designed to "make us good". Neither would we accept any stories with characters or a background that were too familiar. It was no use his beginning:

"Once upon a time there was a little boy and a little girl who lived in Arundel Square, North seven." We wanted fairies, princesses, witches, genii, giants, ogres, goblins, gnomes; primeval forests, deserts, oceans, golden palaces, tents and log huts, pictures in the fire and in the clouds, ivory castles and falling off a rainbow that went out like a light. We had all of these.

My paternal grandmother had died before I was born. She married twice and, during years of widowhood, supported herself and her first family by making ties, by hand, and bright paper flowers, which she carried through the streets on a long pole. My uncle on my mother's side had succeeded in getting himself into the Civil Service so that my father's relatives, though they were legion, we did not know so well. According to my mother's standards, they were "not superior".

My mother censored the stories, too, and many a wild bird of fancy was trapped and slaughtered, at birth, by a shake of the head, a frown and the firm veto, "Not at bedtime."

My mother had a theory, shared by many, that it was frightening tales at bedtime that caused my nightmares. I remember them and know the cause to have been deeper. I think they were not dreams in the sense that there were no pictures, no "essential situation"; they were a feeling, the re-living of a primitive horror.

As an adult, I had these "dreams" again and woke from them, having leapt out of bed, to feel myself standing on the carpet with every wire-fine nerve sticking out through my skin, like cilia, generating fear. As a child I had shouted, and the shouts ringed outwards as the walls pressed in. As an adult I was pregnant and must have been born a score of times while awaiting the birth of my child.

In the beginning, I suppose, we were poor, but not very, not so that we suffered any real deprivation. As I first remember, there were only my brother and I, besides my mother and father, and we lived in two rooms on the first floor of a house in Arundel Square. There was the "front room" which was "best" and the kitchen where we lived. The front room contained a large double bed, two cots, a piano with its stool, a large sofa with one end that let down, two large armchairs to match, a pedestal

13

table with an oval, polished walnut top and claw legs, an octagonal table with a polished mahogany top, four legs with diagonal stretchers supporting a small tray, four high-backed dining-room chairs, upholstered to match the sofa, an oak wardrobe and a vast mahogany chest of drawers. Over the fire-place was a looking-glass, Gothic in structure, with several small shelves, flanking the central large mirror. In front of this was a great gilt clock on an ebony pediment. Gilt cupids supported the blue enamel face of the clock, which slept under a glass case. On either side of the clock were two candlesticks, also gilded and of the same design. The candlesticks were branched and their glass cases precluded any candles being set into them. There was a pair of flesh-coloured vases, each about two feet in height, with ladies in classical dress painted on them, and a number of pieces of Doulton ware reposed between. Two windows opened on to a balcony overlooking the square. The windows were curtained, first with thick lace and then with red serge and plush. On the floor, in front of each window, stood two ceramic pots the size of small barrels, and these contained the aspidistras. From the walls, with their strongly patterned paper, some sturdily framed etchings looked down on us.

All of these things show that, in the beginning, we were not so very poor.

There was red and green linoleum on the floor and thin, flat, patterned rugs. The room was a jumble of ornaments, chamber-pots, toys and pyjamas, Sunday tea, paper bags of sweets and the smell of sunshine on dust. It was our best room all the same.

The kitchen was different and, although we spent most of our lives in it, I do not remember it so well. There was a large sink, in one corner, with a single cold-water tap. Every kind of wash-ing was done at the sink and around it were gathered towels and tea-towels, face-flannels, dish-cloths, medicines and tea-leaves. Under the sink were floor-cloths, rubbish, pipes, disgust and fascination.

The focus of life in the kitchen was the big black range. In winter, the fire was relit by my father every morning. He was an early riser and used to say that bed was a place to die in. If that were so, then it was the one aspect of death that I liked. In winter we always had hot water because kettles rested permanently on top of the stove. There was a big brass fire-guard in front. We had a gas-cooker too, but this was used only when we had no fire. In the centre of the room was a large kitchen table, over the top of which was nailed some "oil cloth" which I used to pick, so that patches of the thin cotton backing showed through and got covered with grime.

Oddly enough, what I remember most about the table were the sounds of it. My mother used to chop vegetables, holding the point of a knife and moving the handle rapidly up and down. I would dance to this sound, running on tip-toe as fast as I could, till the floor shook, the windows rattled, flakes fell from the ceiling and the lady downstairs came up to complain. The sewing-machine, as it made the table vibrate, was better for dancing, slower and more dignified and, after a while, bright scraps of material and ends of cotton would appear on the floor and I would stop dancing to gather these "flowers".

We played another game when the floor was washed. We had to sit with our feet up until parts of the floor were dry. Islands appeared and we could tread on them. They grew, joined and formed continents and soon the whole world was dry again and we could walk where we chose.

In this house, my favourite amenity, and one not often enjoyed, was the verandah. On it my mother grew bulbs in pots. I spent a pleasant half-hour one autumn, taking out these "onions" and throwing them at people below. It was better still in the following spring and summer when, in spite of this treatment, the hyacinths bloomed and the regal lilies nodded down at the street.

My brother, I think, was a fairly obedient child, not only to my parents but, when he was very young, to me too. Unfortunately nobody would believe that he was able to do half the things I taught him and I was nearly always blamed for having done them myself.

We were not often left alone, except on Monday mornings. The wash-house was far down in the basement. There was a big stone copper with a fire-space tunnelled under it. Occasionally we went down. The fire glowed like a jewel and the copper bubbled, belching scalding steam. My own contribution was to put in a red knitted tie of my brother's and our sheets were pink for months. Water ran down the walls, and the wash-house, which smelt of soap, coke and fungi, was full of heat and moisture. Usually we stayed upstairs.

One Monday, while we were thus unsupervised, I became interested in a huge saucepan which I guessed was full of Irish stew. I persuaded my brother to lift it on to the floor. The saucepan was heavy and the gas-stove high, but he managed it quite well. My mother, entering the room to find us standing with pieces of meat and potato clutched in our fists, the jelly oozing through our fingers, refused to believe that it was he who had lifted the saucepan and not I.

When possible the washing was dried in the garden. I do not remember this garden; we probably never went into it. If the weather was wet, the washing was dried on the fire-guard and on lines in the kitchen. The sheets were hung up overnight, and my father used to walk into them, when he first entered the kitchen, in the darkness of early morning. During the Indian Frontier wars he had learnt some Hindustani and always used that for swearing.

At this time my father was "in business" with a partner. They ran a garage and sold second-hand cars. Their wives had shares in this too. My father's partner lived in the same street. He had a daughter of my age whom we called "Rene", and two sons a little younger. I was always told that Rene was a nice friend for me, but I did not like her. She was pale and flabby, she never told lies and I did, and when we had sweets she would always have some left, long after I had finished mine. Sometimes she would give me one, but not often, because, she said virtuously, I ought not to eat them so quickly.

Very seldom we went for a ride in a car, once a vast coop of a thing coloured like a banana, and once a modest black one. My father sat at the wheel while my mother rode beside him. One day when we were playing in the street because there was snow on the ground, we saw a strange little sports car parked up the road. It was vermilion in colour and we thought it aggressively flamboyant. The car was open; we had been making snowballs and these we piled on to the seats.

In the evening when my father came home, he told us how he had found the seats of his car sodden, how ruffians had heaped it with snow and how their parents should keep them more firmly in order.

What happened to the garage I do not know. My parents did not believe in letting everyone know their business, and they did not believe in discussing it in front of children. Certain it is that when we moved from Arundel Square, my father was no longer a capitalist.

Lessons began at home. I learnt the names of letters and how to write them with chalk on a slate. As a child I was ambidextrous, but this was not encouraged for fear that I should become left-handed. I learnt to write numbers and to play dominoes. I knitted with two wooden meat skewers and learnt how to gather material on a running thread. We learnt many songs too, besides nursery rhymes. My mother said that people sang not only when they were happy but when they were sad, and all her songs seemed to be of this kind, full of Victorian sentimentality. Her favourite colour was pale mauve and the songs and the colour seemed to be associated. Both were a kind of half-mourning.

Also connected with the songs and this colour of pale lilac was a picture postcard album. I was allowed to look at it sometimes, sitting up at a table, late on an afternoon, and turning the pages with clean hands. The very first objects of my hero worship were the Mauds and the Lilies of the stage as it existed in my mother's young days. A great deal of long, wavy hair was draped round their shoulders. Their eyes looked constipated and their mouths melancholy. I would gaze at one or other of them for minutes on end. There were other kinds of postcard too; some were comic (but decorous), some were of flowers (pansies, forget-me-nots and violets) and some were marvellously "frosted" with tinsel. The majority, however, were of cats; cats coyly entangled in skeins of wool, cats peeping out of the tops of socks, cats in bags, in boots, in boxes, cats wearing hats and jackets and spats, cats lapping milk, spilling milk, watching milk and treading in milk and cats at the goldfish bowl. Of all these, the only picture I really liked was the uncomplicated one of three fluffy kittens, looking at the camera with round eyes; cats *per se*.

The songs that my father sang had nothing to do with lilac or sentiment; they were of the Edwardian music hall. We never learnt them, for, although the tunes were "catchy", the patter was too swift and he could not or would not sing them slowly, but the rattling exuberance of them always made us laugh.

Sometimes my mother tried to make my father sing a different kind of song, while she accompanied him at the piano, but this was never satisfactory. My mother, with justification, said that he did not keep time. A rousing burst of song would be followed by a pregnant pause, during which the piano would give a sketchy indication of things yet to come. It sounded as though each were reading from a different score and one of them had forgotten to turn over, so "My Old Shako" always came to an end more unfortunate than anything imagined by the writer.

School I enjoyed, for lessons in the infant school were always well within my capacity, and I remember crying there only twice; once was at a story about a cat that climbed a tree, after a bird's nest. The cat fell down and it was he who had my sympathy. I did not know any birds.

The other occasion was during the end-of-term display. The whole school was assembled there and many parents. Dance after dance went on, song after song. My mother did not appear. And suddenly, I stopped the proceedings by breaking into a howl. It was not that I wanted my mother, but just that it was all so wonderful and she was not there to see.

The school we went to was in Barnsbury Park, a very short distance away. Part of Arundel Square led into Offord Road and, by crossing this road and walking down a little way, one could see through a gate into some school grounds. This was not our part of the school but was a separate building. The gates seemed always to be locked, as was the gate between these grounds and our school playground. Rumour had it that this was a "silly school", that is a school for those who were mentally defective or educationally subnormal. We never saw those who went there. They seemed to be "let out" much earlier than we were and probably arrived later. The silly school was a somewhat frightening mystery like the "empty" house, in Thornhill Road, that was boarded up, but said to be inhabited, nevertheless.

To reach Barnsbury Park School, from our house, we had to go along Liverpool Road, in which was a tiny "village" grocer's shop with straw on the floor and bulging sacks, millet in bunches, a smell of aniseed and vulgar "sweets" like tiger nuts, lotus pods, Spanish wood and coconut "tobacco", as well as the boiled sweets and halfpenny sherbet dabs that we were allowed to buy. We went up several stone steps to reach this shop, where we were served by an enormously fat man, with a face like a bunch of glass marbles under a tweed cap so thick with grease that the texture of the cloth was quite obliterated.

Next door to the school was a garage. One entrance of it was in Offord Road, almost opposite Arundel Square, and the other entrance was in Barnsbury Park. From one or two of the classrooms it was possible to look down into this garage.

Our school was supposed to be superior and I think the teaching in the infant school must have been good. I went through it quickly and never lost interest. The school was called a "Demonstration School" and new educational theories were given a trial there. Boys and girls were taught together until they left school at fourteen.

Next door, on the other side was Barnsbury Park Central School, the pupils of which wore caps of red and green. Our rival school was in Thornhill Road. They wore brown caps with yellow letters. So did we, but their letters were T.R.S. while ours were B.P.S. We told them theirs stood for "Tommy Rot" and they called us "Best Pork Sausages".

While we lived in Arundel Square we went for a fortnight's holiday each year, once to Westcliff, once to Hastings, once to Margate and once to Brighton. At Hastings there were cliffs and a stony beach. Apart from this and the first sight of the sea from the train I remember very little of these holidays. Only one remains in memory because of the circumstances under which it was taken.

When I was six years old we were taken one Sunday into the country, with a boy named Dudley. While we were playing, I grazed my left knee, which I frequently did. Although the graze and the skin around it was stained green from a plant that I must have slipped on, I said nothing about it. A few days later it swelled slightly, then, the original green stain having been washed off, the swelling became purple, orange and blue.

On the corner of Ellington Street and Westbourne Road was

a chemist whose name was More. He was a neat little man with a stiff white collar, a small fair moustache, precise speech and amazing sureness, sympathy and gentleness. He used to give me a tiny tablet of perfumed soap each Christmas. On a high shelf in his window, were the usual great glass bottles, with decorated stoppers, and filled with liquid in stained-glass colours. Inside were scales with a basket in which babies were weighed. He examined the abscess on my knee and said that it was deep. If it did not disperse by the end of the week, I must have it lanced.

Two days later my temperature rose and the doctor came in the middle of the night. He was a very big man, half Asian, I think, and very well liked by the people in our neighbourhood. I was said to have been delirious. If I was, then I had a lucid interval. I lay on the big double bed, with my head at the foot. There were newspapers and a towel under me while, above, the gas-light flared, hissing gently within fluted glass shades, rose coloured.

My mother could not bear it and had run out of the house. My screams reached her all the same, although she was deaf in one ear. I felt grieved and somewhat indignant, not so much at the operation but because my father and the doctor held me so ruthlessly.

Dr. Ambrose came every day for a week and pressed my abscess. He stayed to joke about it afterwards and, although I always cried when he came, I always laughed before he went. When it was no longer necessary for him to come, I went to Westcliff, alone, with my mother, where I was wheeled about in a hired pushchair and we were both able to convalesce.

When I was seven I advanced to my father the theory that all of suffering is a punishment for past sins. He said: "Oh pigeon, whatever do you think you had done to deserve that abscess?" But I was convinced that the accumulation of all my small sins would balance it. Ten years later I found the theory in a book on philosophy, but, by then, I had ceased to believe in it.

Before we left this house, my brother and I grew too big for our cots and had to share a single bed. This was put in the kitchen because no amount of ingenuity could have got it into the front room. It was after this that my father had pneumonia.

Some months later, we moved to Ellington Street. It was a

great improvement. Here we were "downstairs", two of our rooms being on the ground floor from the street. The kitchen and living-room were in the basement and there was a scullery and a smaller room on a level with this and the back garden. We had our own lavatory which seemed a waste of space, for it was large enough to put a bed in. My brother and I used it for secret discussions.

The amount of furniture that we brought with us did not seem inadequate in the four rooms we now had. The only two pieces which I do not remember in Arundel Square were a large oak sideboard and a dressing-table, but they may have been there.

It must have been when I was about nine years old that I was in the street, sitting on a step and listening to some older girls talking. They whispered, until one of them became loud with indignation. They were talking about the "lady" who, I suppose, was the relieving officer. I had a feeling that my mother would not approve of my listening nor even of my knowing about it. My family were "superior". That was a good thing to be, but if you wanted to remain in that state, you had to be very careful; ignorance of some things was part of it.

"She said to my mother, 'You've got a gold wedding ring on your finger. You could sell that, couldn't you?' "

There were outraged gasps from the older girls. I would have gasped too but I did not want them to notice me, or they might start whispering again. All the same I understood that there was something very bad about a woman being told to sell her wedding ring. It was mystic and terrible. Mrs. Morrall, down the road, had once pawned hers and had to sleep on the sofa in her front room until she got it back again. After that, of course, she could sleep in bed with her husband like everybody else.

"My mother said to her, she said, 'You've got a row of beads round your neck but I've got the arms of my children.' "

It seemed then to be the perfect answer, a wonderful, beautiful answer, but, when I was much older and thought back on this, it seemed that the full consequences of selling the ring might not have been so bad after all.

I went home and told my mother, but she was not impressed

and did not approve of my listening to "that sort of talk". All the same I was disturbed and dreamed of a woman with a lot of children like tadpoles, all hanging round her neck on very long thin arms.

This incident was related to the Means Test but I did not know that then. My parents never adopted the attitude of the Hunger Marchers, although we were probably as hungry as anyone. To them there was something shameful about being unemployed, and for years we children did not know it was to that class that we belonged. To my parents the powers that be were right, however things worked out.

This is the only such incident that I remember, but I think that, nevertheless, I absorbed the atmosphere of those times, for, although I have since known many social workers, personally, and liked them, yet the fear and antagonism which I feel at the thought of official interference with the private loves and the private lives of individual people leave no doubt as to where I belong.

I was said to have brains and probably more than a pottle, but they were not of a very reliable kind and did not include common sense. As well as these I had large green eyes, a protuberant mouth, full of black teeth, and curly brown hair, this last evidently inherited from my father, since my mother had only what she called "nine hairs and a bit of cotton". As for clothes I was not so much dressed as decently covered by garments produced, through what must have been miraculous contrivance, by my mother. But there seemed to be something about me that instantly weakened any elastic that I wore, and my legs, in their spiralling stockings, looked like conch shells. I rarely had a button missing, in the strict sense of the word, since I put them in my pocket, when they came off, but many were retained only by will-power and a single thread. Also I was nearly always very far from where I was meant to be, and when I tried to get from one place to another in less than no time, there followed me, always some inches behind, a bedraggled blue bow, invisibly attached by one or two long hairs. It was my familiar, a sleazy, blue butterfly, and, in its way, it symbolised my tenuous hold on reality.

Since I was the eldest, my aquaintance with the streets began fairly late. There were no older children whom my mother would trust to look after me and besides, we were superior to so many of our neighbours. We were snobs in our way. Although we were hungry poor my mother never went out of the house in bedroom slippers or with an apron rolled up under her coat, and my father wore a collar and tie on Sundays, not the spotless white "choker" which most of the men affected. We were not "posh" since we never wore anything but clothes that were very plain indeed, or worse, and those who did looked down on us, as we looked down on the aprons and chokers.

Our "superiority" demanded, also, a way of living that was almost monastic in its strictness. It was slovenly, for instance, to do the week's washing on any day of the week but Monday, snobbish to send it "out". It was slovenly to have the midday meal later than one o'clock and snobbish to call it anything but "dinner". It was slovenly to run round to local shops on just any day of the week; it was snobbish to buy flowers. My mother's chief characteristic was an unremitting, lifeless energy. She had a thin mouth and tired eyes, like dents in a tin.

Soon after I was first allowed to go out to play alone I wandered down the street and found it deserted by any who were young enough to be of any use. Probably most of the other children were still having their dinners, after I had finished mine. Being superior had its drawbacks. If there had been anyone at all, whether I knew them or not, I would have gone up and offered them a "go" with my skipping rope or asked for a bite of their apple or a suck of their gob-stopper. This last was an extremely hard, round ball that would fit into one's mouth like an egg into an egg-cup. Each was dyed in layers of very bright colour, purple, nigger pink and poison green. You took the gob-stopper out of your mouth, at intervals, sometimes in order to speak and sometimes to see what colour it had now become. Gob-stoppers were "common". I was not allowed to buy one. I was not allowed even to pronounce the word. My only hope was to get a lick of somebody else's.

But there was no one in the street. I kicked around for some time and then it occurred to me to go for a walk. Somebody had told me that if you went first to the right, then to the left and so on, inexorably alternating right and left-hand turnings, you could go quite a long way into strange parts and always be able to find your way back again. I felt that this was a good idea, although I realised that I had not fully grasped the system. What I had grasped was that the system for getting back again would be different, but I did not doubt that I should be able to work it out when I tried. I set off, found a stick and rattled it on other people's railings as I passed. Ralph Roberts's father, who was on night work, came out and shook his fist at me, but he had had to stop to put his trousers on, over his pyjamas, and I was a long way past his house by then.

Now I realise that I can only have turned twice, left along Offord Road, right along Liverpool Road and left again down Park Street, but it seemed a long way and I had crossed Liverpool Road. The pavement in Park Street was broken up by very small cobbled "roads". They were probably "entrances" for commercial vans. This meant that one continually stepped down off the pavement and up again. It made the way seem much longer.

I certainly got somewhere, but grew frightened before my surroundings became strange. I was only in Upper Street, which I knew well, but it was a "busy" road. I had never been there alone before. People, hurrying by, nearly pushed me over, as I stared vacantly at the traffic, which seemed to be moving in much the same way, and I did not want to be "jostled" by a tram.

I suddenly felt no more than the six-years-old that I was. I had always been told, "If ever you are lost, don't go with a stranger; find a policeman."

He was very tall and it made my arm ache, holding his hand. The people who had brushed past me, before, now began to notice me.

"Poor little thing! She's lost. Poor little thing!"

The policeman must have been going off duty, for we walked, at my pace, to the police station. There I sat on a bench with my feet swinging and policemen, without helmets, came and looked at me. My policeman had very fair hair, almost white. I had decided that I would be afraid of an albino so I asked him if he had pink eyes. He stooped down, smiling, and it was all right. They were blue. Another policeman took me home. In the police station they had given me a bar of chocolate and an apple. The chocolate cost a penny. I kept the wrapper for a long time to show that I too was sometimes able to have this chocolate, thin as a biscuit, very milky and far superior to the sweets we bought for a halfpenny and that were screwed up in squares of newspaper. It was a new experience too, to have a whole apple to myself, since I was always told that I could not eat a whole one and would waste it. It occurred to me, when I had eaten nearly all of this apple, that I might have saved the core just to show what I could do, when given the chance. The stalk was no use for this, so I threw it away. As soon as I was on the doorstep and realised that I had been lost, I burst into tears.

This did not happen the second time. I knew the way to the police station now. Many of the children round our way had been taught to run from the police and never to answer questions. At school they taught that a policeman was a friend and nobody believed it, any more than they spoke at home in the accents recommended by the teachers. We were superior because my parents had the same attitude about police as had the teachers, so I had no hesitation about going to the police station again, and that time I got a custard tart and a fancy cake. They were "shop-bought" and they were neither broken nor stale. Policemen without helmets came and looked at me again but they were not the same ones. I pouted and sucked in my cheeks. They took me as far as the corner of the street and then I said I was all right and ran on. I was jubilant. I had gone to the police station intending to be "a poor little thing" and it had worked. It was my first experience of deliberately and successfully "putting on an act".

But, the third time, I knew the game was up, as soon as I went in. The fair policeman met me and smiled. He did not say anything but went through a green painted door. After a moment a gust of laughter came out and then another policeman. He told me to go home. I sucked in my cheeks, made my eyes large and stared up at him, but it was no use. I stood on the corner looking at the police station saying to myself that I was lost. I was. After a while I went home.

# CHAPTER II

# AN ALBINO GOLLIWOG *

I NEVER liked dolls—teddy bears and monkeys, but not my
dolls. I believe I must actively have disliked them, for almost
the only game I ever played with them was to hang them up
round the room and hit them with a stick as I passed. The only
exception to this was the baby doll, named Bobby. He had a
calico trunk, very firmly stuffed with straw, and a papier mâché,
pock-marked face. He wore long baby clothes to hide the fact
that he had no legs and he was wrapped in a shawl because he had
no arms either. The back of his head was missing too, and he had
to wear a bonnet stuffed with paper. I loved him because of his
terrible mutilation. That I, myself, had, at some time been the
cause of his deprivations probably did not occur to me; or perhaps it did and my exaggerated love was a form of atonement.

One day during the summer holiday, when rain hung like
cage-wire all round the house, I determined to make a golliwog.
I decided on a golliwog because I knew that I was not very
skilled, so that whatever I made would probably look comical
and I could think of nothing but a golliwog that was meant to
look so.

I waited until our mother was a little less busy than usual
then I asked if I could have a bit of stuff.

"A piece of material, dear," said our mother, "not a bit of
stuff," and she went to the large bottom drawer which was
rather like a rag-bag and began to look through her "pieces".

These were all classified and neatly tied in bundles. All the
remains of past sewing were there, beautiful pieces from years
and years ago when you could buy bags of rich remnants from
Liberty's and the bottom drawer had been something quite
different. Bundles of such fabrics nestled against others, the
parts of garments worn and worn again and then unpicked and
washed and pressed and laid away until they should be needed.

But I could not make a golliwog of Indian muslin and I did not want one with flowers all over him, like a skin disease. Even a golliwog could not look as funny as that.

In the end my mother lost patience, brought out a piece of sheeting and, shutting the drawer, said: "Then you may have that. It's all there is."

"But it's white!" I exclaimed hopelessly.

"It's a lovely piece of material," answered our mother, "pure linen and very strong."

My father said: "I've heard of white negroes in Africa. They're called albinos and they have red hair."

I could make a fuss. I was capable of making a fuss for hours. But if I did, I should get no help, the wonderful, wet afternoon would be spoilt and I should get no black stuff anyway. Besides, although I might have been afraid of an albino policeman, the idea of making an albino golliwog was not unattractive, especially when my mother offered me an old woollen glove which I could unravel to make beautiful, curly red hair.

When he was finished, he looked quite presentable. He had two pink glass buttons for eyes and his hair was brilliant.

Outside the family the first person to see "Alby" was the sweep. He came regularly down our road and so did the window-cleaner. I am sure we never employed either of them, but the sweep always spoke to me. Now he looked at what I was nursing in my lap. As he did so, his face dropped.

"What an extraordinary thing!" he exclaimed. "What is it?"

"It's a golliwog," I said.

"No!" said the sweep. "Golliwogs are black."

"This one's white," I answered. "He's an albino."

"A what!" His mouth flew open and he roared with horrible, excluding, grown-up laughter. He laughed so much he could hardly stand up and had to hold on to the railings. He laughed till the tears came into his eyes and made little pink runnels in the soot on his cheeks.

Just then Pat Loony's mother opened the door. She was so plump that she sagged shapelessly, like a rubber balloon filled with water, although Pat was one of the smallest children I have known.

The sweep said: "Ever seen an albino golliwog?"

Mrs. Loony shook her head and her cheeks went on shaking by themselves after her head had stopped. She chuckled. "That kid's a caution."

I did not mind being a caution. Quite often I did not mind being laughed at, but this was not one of those times. I became very sentimental over Alby. Once I found him sitting in front of a mirror on the mantelpiece. His head drooped and, when I took him down, his face seemed longer than ever. Our mother said it was because he had too little stuffing, but I knew that the poor creature did not like himself at all and there could be nothing more wonderfully melancholy than this. Later, when some black stuff did become available, I refused it angrily.

Sound material was never easily come by in our household. Many of the clothes we wore were bought in the Caledonian Market. None of them were ever sent to the cleaners. Those that were washable were washed and those that were not were washed just the same. My mother once bought six yards of material for a halfpenny. It had been in a fire and was scorched and burned. We got a dress out of the whole bits and I won a prize at a fancy-dress party, as Cinderella, wearing the rest of it.

In Islington, where we lived, anything but wool was discounted as clothing. Nothing else had any warmth in it. All of us children wore many layers and must have looked like teddy-bears or those pin-cushions that are made by winding strips of felt layer upon layer.

Apart from all this there were some cotton garments which were worn not for warmth but as protection against dirt of one kind or another. The material for these came from the meat market, at Smithfield, where one of my uncles was a bummaree. After being discarded by pieces of pork and beef and mutton, it went to clothe us. The meat market material was of two kinds; first there was the ordinary "meat-cloth", a kind of unbleached knitted stuff which was somewhat elastic. All our face-cloths, dish-cloths and floor-cloths were made of it and, because of its high powers of absorbence, it was of great use on the babies.

The other material was from the packing-cases and was a kind of loosely woven checked gingham, rather of the texture of a fine flour-bag but in various unfortunate colours, so that we were always to be seen in overalls of black and white over-checked with liquorice brown, bilious green, jaundiced yellow or livid mauve.

The things which I shall never forget were the sub-standard stockings. They really were sub-standard. Sometimes they were extremely short and would not keep up, sometimes one was longer than the other, some, which were worse, were of two colours and textures, changing somewhere about the middle of the leg where it could not possibly be made to look like a matter of choice. But the worst, the very dreadful worst, were those with seams up the front.

One day, having just come out of school, I was walking along by the shops with two of my best friends, when I saw my mother coming towards us and carrying a shopping-bag in each hand. My mother was wearing stockings with seams up the front, and the next moment I found myself doing something I had never intended to do; I grabbed my friends, one by each hand, and saying, "Quick, run!" darted with them through the crowd.

Afterwards I thought I should never get over the shame of it. Nobody at home would speak to me but the cat who was too young to understand. They thought it was because I was too lazy to help to carry home the shopping and I could not explain to anyone that it was because of the stockings with seams up the front, so I sat under the Judas tree in the church gardens and added tears to the other stains that were on Alby.

Meals at our house were unusual affairs, for each piece of crockery was unique in its way, the plates and cups and saucers being throw-outs from a pottery. Some was actually thrown out on to a rubbish-dump and we retrieved it, not much chipped. Soon, however, the factory owners got to know that this stuff had a market value. It ceased to appear on the dumps and arrived instead on the market stalls, most of it bearing extra-ordinary coloured blobs which the unknowing would try to scrape off their plates or fish out of their cups. Sometimes the plates or saucers rocked on the table; sometimes a cup was off balance and, like an old-fashioned tumbler, had to be held upright until it was empty.

We had our useful "contacts" too, amongst people in the

neighbourhood. One of them used to get bread at wholesale prices and sugar a farthing a pound cheaper than retail. The week-end joint came straight from Smithfield. We knew somebody who worked for a builder who was getting rid of some paint that he couldn't sell because it was such an unpopular colour. After that, nearly everything in our house was painted the same rather disgusting yellow, mustard laced with Worcester sauce. At one time, our father worked in a soap factory. Nobody would have thought that anyone working in such a clean-sounding job could have smelt as peculiar as he did. He, too, could get a commodity at wholesale prices, but perhaps we did not value it sufficiently to be willing to pay for it. Instead, we used an extraordinary waste product which was brought home like pease pudding in sheets of newspaper. It was whitish green, soft and sticky and, kept in jars or saucers by the kitchen sink, was used almost exclusively. With hot water, it produced a stiff glutinous lather which it was impossible to rinse off entirely; in cold water it merely slithered over one's skin. But at least we had made a gesture towards cleanliness and we felt we were not quite beyond the pale.

High, black, spiked railings surrounded Arundel Square and lindens with sooty boles and a sticky excrescence from their leaves stood there, as though they had been waiting for years to get out. Groups of disconsolate privet waited too, round the feet of the lindens, like children, with black-trousered adults, in a funeral group. When it rained the pavement under the trees was slippery with black slime and always the place smelt of cats. I had not then become aware of the scent of linden blossom. Perhaps these lindens never flowered. The only good smell about the square was the autumn one of heaped leaves smouldering.

Within the railings were no flowers, but gravel paths, rank grass and two tennis-courts. On one side of the square were the allotments and the railway. Even after we moved to Ellington Street, I used to go back to the square to play. We had no key to it by then, but I was used to "climbing over".

Once in my life I made what I felt to be a large contribution to the food of the family, but it cost me dear. I had always thought that if ever I climbed the railings by the railway I should instantly be run over by a train and I was about eight before I managed to do it. Once over, I noticed some strange plants. I had never seen anything like them before. I pulled one up and found a carrot on the end of it. I started to pull them up as fast as I could, using both hands. I got onions, turnips, beetroots, potatoes and a cabbage. I had no pockets, but I wore some voluminous bloomers. They had been cut down for me and I hated them. I prayed that the elastic would hold and stuffed all the vegetables into these. Running frantically through the streets on skinny little legs and desperately clutching my sagging, bulging stomach, I must have looked like a little alley cat about to have kittens.

When I got home I hid all the vegetables in the scullery. They were not found until I was in bed. My parents were not in favour of stealing, but I did not get into trouble. My father found me in tears and thought that anyone as remorseful as that had been punished enough. I had, but it wasn't remorse. It was only that, when I undressed, I found a large green caterpillar crawling on my skin.

As for other things necessary to near normal, civilised existence, it was "just a question of knowing". There was a "cut-price" shop at the other end of the main street, and there you could save as much as a shilling on the week's shopping by paying careful attention to prices. And there was the Caledonian Market on Tuesdays and Fridays. This was a cattle market on other days of the week and the cattle-pens made intriguing gymnastic apparatus during school holidays.

Our treats were inexpensive too, for, mostly, we went on picnicking expeditions, perhaps very seldom, but they live, in memory, as days which changed the whole of our lives and all our summers were coloured by them. We took thick sandwiches, sour apples, carefully halved, and bottles of water.

There were some woods and, surely, they were at Highgate? I now know people who live at Highgate and I cannot think that the woods were then so near. The ground was soft and leaf-mouldy and I was constantly disappointed because there were no bluebells. There never could be any bluebells, for, whenever we went, the trees had been long in leaf and it was much too late in the year, but how could we know this, we who, moved by the desire to perpetuate ourselves, stole wet cement which we pressed on to a wall to cut our names in.

But, at Totteridge, there were buttercups, an abundance, a wealth, a waste of buttercups, like gold lifted clear of the ground in an outpouring of joy. When it really came to it, in spite of our constant preoccupation with tales of exploration and high adventure, we never went farther than two open fields away. How could we? There were more flowers than we could pick in just one, and we spent all day gathering and gathering. It was like trying to clear the seashore of sand. There was so much and we would not be able to come again for such a long time. It was pain to look back at that vast abandonment of wealth which ordinary, childish, physical limitations forbade our taking away.

Sometimes we went fishing. We had relatives who lived near the Wanstead Flats. My mother said that this was almost "East End" and not superior. These relatives belonged to the darker side of the family and I do not know how they were connected. They wore chokers and bedroom slippers. They were always extremely kind to us children and my mother was always extremely aloof towards them. Each year they would bring us a piece of Christmas pudding and we gave them a piece of ours. Their pudding was the colour of brown paper and tasted faintly bitter, as though there were carbolic in it.

Every time you ate a piece of somebody else's Christmas pudding it was the guarantee of one happy month in the coming year. To refuse it was as unlucky as wiping off a kiss. My mother used to shudder as she swallowed the smallest piece possible.

All their food tasted horrible, but we were always too hungry to mind very much, and in our own street lives we often consumed worse. (We picked and ate the soft leaves of linden trees and stole lumps of pitch to put in our mouths. This was as good as chewing gum, once it softened, although it tasted oddly.) My mother told us that we "didn't want to go there", but we did, and when they came to see us and invited us to their house, at some unspecified time, I learned, as I got older, to insist on fixing the date so that we really did go. This occurred at most twice a year, but the pleasure from it ran through all the summer.

The flats were probably just a fetid marsh. To us they were a lake. This lake was so shallow that nowhere did the water come higher than one's thighs (except accidentally), and the lake was so vast that it was possible to stand in it and see around only a sheet of water and a thin line of moth-eaten grass in the distance. Children stood in couples dotted all about, like birds, and the mud was ankle deep.

Frightened sticklebacks buried themselves in the mud and their spines stuck into bare feet. Every so often a child would raise one foot, pick off a tiddler and pop it into the jar which hung round his neck. The real fishing was done with an onion sack; two people held the ends and, stooping, walked along with it taut between them in the water. Together they lifted the sack; the sticklebacks escaped with the water and the mud, leaving the angrily whiskered gudgeon jumping about like cats on hot bricks. We caught snails and a huge fresh-water mussel.

The blessed peace did not last long, for my brother and I often quarrelled and there came the inevitable moment when neither would carry back the sack alone. We each held a corner and stared obstinately at one another. Little waves slapped our rolled-up clothes with gentle malice.

"If you let go," said my brother, "so shall I."

Then, as if in answer to a prayer, there floated towards us, out of the reeds, a shallow box. It bobbed there with sinister suggestiveness.

"We could float it back in the box," said my brother.

We picked up the sack and twisted out most of the water. I put Alby in the box first to give him a ride. Then we put the folded sack on top of him and the whole lot sank.

I hesitated not at all before I held my nose, shut my eyes, and plunged. For a moment, the only part of me that was above the surface was the part that was already wet from the malicious little waves. Alby was sorrier than ever when I brought him up and I was a sorry sight myself. My brother had a way of laughing very deeply and quite silently. His face screwed up so that only the tears that squeezed themselves out, as though from slits in a lemon, showed where his eyes were. He shook so rapidly that he seemed to be still. My brother laughed in the way that a top spins.

"Never mind!" he said at last, in a tiny pip of a voice that seemed to be shaken out of him. "You'll dry in the sun."

He was in a good mood, since I had managed to rescue the sack which was precious, for it was difficult to persuade a greengrocer to give you one when all you ever bought from him was a few pennyworths' of pot-herbs and some potatoes; also he had been "good", while I should obviously be in big trouble when I got home. However well I dried out, I could not disguise what had happened to me, and Alby looked even worse than before, the parts of him that had been white being now a dismal khaki. The mud was so sticky and opaque that, when we came out of the water, we were wearing socks of it. While we were unsuccessfully trying to remove this, I noticed something which made me think that I was dreaming.

Near the bank were a few stunted water-lily leaves and, seated on one of them, a frog no larger than a little finger-nail. It was the sort of thing one read about but never saw, like bluebells, the sort of thing one only half believed in, like elves and squirrels and wild rabbits and God. These things belonged to books, not to real life. But then, looking minutely into the grass about us we saw dozens—hundreds of these little brown frogs, swarming, like cockroaches.

For a moment we played with the idea of emptying the jar of fish and taking home the frogs instead. We would never find another jar, for these, returned to the grocer, were worth a halfpenny each. At last we found a cardboard cigarette box and filled it with wet weed and tiny frogs.

Being wet seemed to have made me tired, and I sat in the bus half asleep and looking at the pattern on the upholstered seats and then at the slatted floor. I noticed something like a large insect crawling along and thought how strange it was to see a spider in a bus. I wondered why one never did. There were no cobwebs either. While I was looking dreamily at this spider, it suddenly hopped. It was a frog.

The box in my brother's pocket was open and all the frogs were coming out. There they were, when one looked closely, on the seats, on the floor, on people! We tried to gather them up, unobtrusively, but the thin lady behind us began to make a fuss and the conductor came to see. He turned us off the bus, and what happened to the frogs that were left behind we never knew.

We had to walk so far and were so late getting home that the police had been informed and our father was out looking for us when we arrived. I think it was the last time we ever went to the flats.

These things, the buttercups, the little fish, the frogs, were free, or nearly so, although the value of them was undoubted, for they were "free" in more senses than one. There was so little else that we could have and hold that was not inevitably associated with a rather desperate financial contrivance; nevertheless, even this was not always disagreeable to me. It seemed to give zest to our lives.

The happiest shopping was that done between seven o'clock and eight on a Saturday night in the Chapel Street market. For me it meant staying up long past my bedtime, and this added to the excitement. We bought a bagful of stale cakes for a penny and pounds of broken biscuits, congratulating ourselves on the fact that, but for the passing of a day or two and some slight accidents, our purchases would have been worth at least twelve times the price.

I remember these evenings always as dark, wet and autumnal. I was allowed to go ostensibly to help to carry home the shopping-bags, but I doubt if I really carried much. My recollection is of being very small and of being comfortably and warmly jostled by the towering crowd about me. I would look up sometimes through a kind of chimney at a dark grape-bloom sky and cold rain would fall on my face. I could feel the pavement through the soles of my shoes and I always imagined the cold as "striking up" inimically, like electricity. The steam from old damp clothes hung above us like gauze, coloured orange by the light of the naphthalene flares. I have always liked the smell of old damp clothing for the memories it evokes.

The feeling of excitement grew as the evening progressed. The people in charge of the stalls shouted more and more raucously. The men seemed to be ferrety little fellows, but the women were twice as large and twice as loud. They wore men's caps and I found them frightening, possibly because of their methods in dealing with the swarms of children who rummaged in the shavings in the road, looking for rotten fruit. We were not allowed to do this. We were poor, but we had our standards.

On the face of the post office clock the minute hand climbed towards the hour. The crowd kept moving without getting anywhere. The women shuffled along, most of them clutching purses in coarse ungloved hands. Once they caught a pickpocket and there was great shouting. I thought I would much rather have been in charge of a policeman than at the mercy of those women.

It was five minutes to eight and people began to leave the market, but we didn't. Once I caught the eye of a woman in a cap and her eyes said, "I know what you are doing", and I smiled complacently because I knew too. Some of the stalls were packing up, but not those with perishable goods. The naphtha flares roared, their flames like tattered orange banners blown upward by the wind. It was warm beneath them. It seemed miraculous that they didn't set fire to everything. The shining rain slanted through the light. The voices of the remaining stall-holders grew frantic. Nobody looked at price tickets now.

We listened to those voices: "Twopence a pound! Come on! Lovely plums. Lovely, lady! Twopence a pound!"

They were not lovely. They were half rotten. By Monday they would be no use at all. A policeman on the corner was watching to see that nothing was sold after eight. Two minutes to go. The prices began their asymptotic progression towards zero. Twopence. A penny. A halfpenny. My mother nodded and fished some coppers out of her purse. Her lips were tight with the strain of it all. But the stall-holders were past caring or weighing anything. Into our bags they shovelled pounds and pounds of fruit because there was now nothing else to be done with it.

We passed the policeman on the corner. It was a long way home, and cold now, away from the crowd. Brilliantly lit buses went bowling past us, and we hurried, almost running. There was a thrilling urgency about it. The fruit was so perilously near to complete decomposition that it seemed that the quantity that might be saved diminished with every moment.

At last we were home, in the gaslight, we children sitting up round the large table and cutting the bad parts out of the fruit with old sharp knives. The rest we balanced by guesswork against the sugar and tipped it into the huge old pan.

It was dreadfully late. My eyes were closing by themselves. But I didn't want to go to bed. The tins were ready. Soon the pan would be lifted on to the stove. I always felt that we had reached the very height of creative achievement when the house was filled with the smell of boiling jam.

The sight of it was beautiful too. The darkness of it glowed and a fragrant heat came up. If I waited long enough I might be able to eat some of the sweet pink scum that rose to the surface. As I stirred and savoured the smell I forgot Alby whom I carried always stuffed into the front of my checked pinafore, and the next thing I knew was that he too was in the pan and gazing up at the kitchen ceiling with a rather irritating, sub-human innocence.

I whisked him out and sponged him quickly. The stickiness came off but not the fruit juice, and Alby, on top of everything else, was stained with uneven patches of purplish red. I dared not let anyone see him and I could not leave the jam. I stuffed him, wet as he was, up the leg of my knickers and climbed back on the chair by the gas-stove. As soon as I could I ran out into the dark passage to put Alby into the pocket of my coat. I did not dare to take him to bed again for fear that someone should see him and guess what had happened. I knew that I should have a guilty feeling every tea-time until the last of that year's damson jam was eaten. Had I known myself better I would have realised that never in this world could I keep so dark a secret for long, that, inevitably the tension would become so acute that it would begin to stick out, like a toe through a sock, and the unsavoury facts be wrung from me.

It was about this time that my Aunt Maud died. This was not the first death I had known, for my maternal grandparents died when I was four. I was told merely that I should never see them again, but I knew they were dead. My sadness lasted perhaps twenty minutes. After that I forgot. With Aunt Maud it was different. We were older now. I knew when the letter came, with the black border round the envelope. We waited while my mother opened the letter. Then she told us and burst into tears. My mother is not Irish but she could keen.

Grief did not come then. I was merely shocked at my mother's outburst. For mourning, my mother had her old coat dyed. One went into mourning then, at the loss of a relative, for months or a year or two. My mother often dyed faded garments or soft furnishings, and this was another thing that helped to make us a little more respectable than most. Now she looked at the big stone copper and her spirit failed. She had no other coat.

Perhaps my uncle helped with "the mourning" for his job was secure and he was so much better off than we were. However it was, my mother embarked on the unprecedented venture of having her coat dyed by the cleaners on the corner. There was a special quick service for mourning.

Aunt Maud was related to us only by marriage, being the wife of my mother's only brother. Her daughter was two years older than I and her son two years older than that. The latter I worshipped and with the former I exchanged secrets, although the really revelatory ones were always from her. As soon as we met we talked about dying. She told me how, on her deathbed, my aunt had asked to see her children, but was too near to death to be able to distinguish between them. They said good-bye and her voice was very weak.

My cousin and I sat bolt upright on the sofa and stared at each other; our eyes and our throats ached with dry, unchildish weeping. We were rigid with grief.

My cousin said: "I'm terrified of death."

I was too, and we sat there knowing that one day it would have to come.

I said to my cousin: "What would your father say if he knew we talked about it?"

"He would send you home and never let you come again."

The secret of death was then the guiltiest one of all.

When I got home I could not find Alby. I could not believe that he was lost, but, when I had to go to bed without him, the sense of bereavement was stronger than anything I had known. Sadness I often enjoyed; this was pain. I could not talk about it, for my mother was in mourning, but I wept and prayed late into the night and awoke to a nightmare feeling of loss. I was lying on my back in the dark. Salt rivulets had stiffened on my face, like the side-pieces of spectacles and, in each ear, lay a little pool of tears.

The day before the funeral, my mother was unpacking her coat in the kitchen. There was a smaller parcel inside the large one and on my mother's weary face an expression I had come to know. Her pleasures were so few. I waited, with my heart on a stalk, until she gave me the small parcel to unwrap. I knew it was Alby because I recognised my sewing and I now knew too that he was the only golliwog in the whole world who was really and truly black, to the last shred of his stuffing.

It was typical of my mother that she should want to do this for me and typical of her, too, that she should have no idea what his temporary loss had meant, nor how the heart in me had been dissolved.

*The word 'golliwog' was not offensive then as it may be now. The classic golliwogs were of old black woollen stockings, and always home-made so that they seemed to be part of ourselves, our family, and, because of this, they were especially loved.
*AR, 1984*

# CHAPTER III

# NO GRASS IN OUR GARDEN

I LEARNT to run before I could walk, but I do not remember it. The technique was similar to that employed by an athletic sprinter: he crouches on all fours, knees half bent and stern in air, the weight of his body, which is thus thrown forward, being taken partly by the tips of his fingers resting on the ground. At the crack of the pistol he draws back his hands, while maintaining his stance, and has to keep running so as not to fall over. At eleven months my mastery of this was imperfect and the experiment ended with my splitting my head on the fender. All the same, as a means of locomotion the technique is not a bad one and I seem to have used a modified form of it for a good many years.

Our house was at the Westbourne Road end of Ellington Street which sloped down towards Liverpool Road. It dipped steeply towards the bottom and the pavement was cracked and uneven where the dip occurred. This part of the street and the lamp-post near it were the scene of most of my minor accidents. It was here that I received nearly all of my visible scars.

Our house boasted a front "garden", and giving entrance to it was a gate which was usually jammed shut. There was a kind of flattened horseshoe instead of a latch. It was rusty and squeaked as the gate was opened or closed. The front garden was quite full of knot grass and this I accepted, for it seemed to me to be a fairly attractive substitute for a lawn and better than mud or dust. It looked down on to an "area" which we called an "airy" and which was protected by a kind of roof of iron railing on which I used to walk, until I slipped once.

It must have been a wonderfully hot, sunny summer's day for, afterwards, I lay, bruised, grazed, oiled and bandaged in the knot grass amidst the smell of petrol fumes, horse dung and tarry dust from the roads. It was only on very hot days that we were ever allowed to do this because of the cold and the damp that would "strike up" from the ground.

The back garden was less pleasant, bare as the asphalt playground at school, but more treacherous, in that it was uneven, packed hard with pebbles in clay. The back of the house was to the north, so that this garden rarely got any sun and was, in any case, not so much shaded as darkened by three of the ubiquitous, sooty, sticky lindens, which rose as tall as the three-storeyed houses at the end of the garden, against the smoke-grimed, crumbling brick wall.

My mother liked the trees because they prevented our being "overlooked" in summer by the inhabitants of Bride Street (how inaptly named!). I did not. I wanted a garden, but, wherever one dug, one came on the spreading roots of the trees, sapping the life out of the ground. The trees seemed to me to be a respectable green screen around the sordid isolation of the garden, themselves precluding any graciousness and beauty that we could be proud to show. I hated these trees and, when I remembered, futilely cut and sawed at the roots.

I wanted a lawn and this seemed possible, for surely a lawn was just grass. So I began to take the garden in hand. Every time I went out I dug up a tuft of grass from somewhere and carried it home, roots and earth and all. This I pressed on to the stony ground and watered. Once I succeeded in making a patch of green about the size of the seat of a kitchen chair. But, either through cats or the sun and the wind, always the lawn ended in the same way, as a few dry scattered tufts, looking like nothing so much as the lumps of matted hair that are dragged from a slut's comb. Grass grew everywhere, even between paving-stones, but it would not grow in our garden.

Then, one autumn, for a few months, my father worked in the gardening department of a large London store and brought home dozens, countless dozens of jonquil bulbs. There was one thing for which my mother would never forgive my father. I overheard her say so. Perhaps it was the bulbs, for, if he bought them, they must have cost quite all of a week's wage. We planted them around the edge of the garden against the dingy walls.

And they came up. April was full of flowers that year and,

above, the lime trees made a delicate rough-cut net that was sewn with leaf buds.

Then, when all the border was quick with jonquils, calculating creatures that we were, we began to count them, so that we could boast of how many we had. There were hundreds, and every day new flowers opened as the early sun shone from the Liverpool Road, along the deep trough, between the houses, to where our garden lay, and we counted again in the late April evenings when the sun had forgotten to go down.

Soon the blooms began to die, we picked them off, the number dwindled and we did not count any more. Something must have happened to them after that, for they did not come up another year and the garden returned to nearly its old form. Only two things were added and those by me; they were a little rockery, under the trees in each of the far corners of the garden. I piled earth there and then managed to procure a number of "rocks" which I pressed into it. They were not really rocks but lumps of concrete with stones embedded. I cannot remember how or when I got them, but they were the kind of thing one sees lying around where roads are being drilled. They must have been heavy and I could not have been very big, for these events all occurred before I was eleven and became too refined for such efforts. The rockeries were useful when we wanted to climb over the wall. Not a leaf ever grew on them.

Steps led up to our front door which was varnished and artificially "grained". By hanging precariously over the area, one could climb from the railings of the top step on to the window-sill of our front room. It was usually possible to prise up the window.

The bedroom occupied by my parents was on the same floor, separated from the front room by large communicating doors which were never opened.

The passage was ours and stairs went up from it to where other people lived. Four stairs went down from it to our own wonderfully large lavatory. At street level, this was the only part of our accommodation that stimulated our imagination. The lavatory had a small window, about eighteen inches square, small enough to be worth aiming at with a ball from the garden, small enough to be excitingly difficult to climb through when we let ourselves down into the garden on a "rope" made from bed-clothes knotted together. We could not do this from any other window, first because the only window at this level and at the back of the house was that of my parents' bedroom. It was only about a six-foot drop from this to the roof of the coal-shed and that was no use, besides, in the lavatory, we could lock ourselves in and thus escape discovery. Once my brother was commanded to come out, but he pushed the bed-clothes through the window to me, in the garden, before he did so.

This ruse was not as successful as it might have been, because we could not help going into fits of laughter over it. We were punished for being "up to something", but our mother never did discover just what it was we were "up to".

We always planned to get out of my parents' bedroom window if ever there were a fire in the night. I cannot think why, because we slept downstairs at the back, at garden level, and if we had been in either of the two rooms on the ground floor, we could have walked out of the front door.

The coal-shed was divided into three, but we did not use our part for coal because, being in the basement, we had a cellar. My brother and I used to play in the shed. For a while it was a zoo and we kept in it all the spiders and caterpillars, tadpoles and fishes that we collected during the summer. We had no idea how to take care of these creatures, and they did not live very long.

For most of the time the shed was a "house". The floor of it was only about a yard square and we found a piece of old coconut matting to put down. Then we brought in all the toy animals and dolls and found boxes for ourselves. After this we did nothing but sit on the boxes, enjoying the closed-in atmosphere of the "house".

The shed soon began to smell strongly of mildew. Our mother said that the mat was probably rotting and we must take it out and air it. Unfortunately we had put it directly on to the earth floor and it was now in a state of disintegration, but worse than this, under the matting was a very large earthworm.

I do not usually mind worms, nor caterpillars, nor slugs, nor harmless snakes, nor anything that crawls. I was not afraid to touch bits of fluff as my brother was, and I was not much afraid of the dark, at least, rarely so much afraid that the fear became uncontrollable and I could not walk into darkness when necessary. But the sight of this particular worm, in the enclosed and secret atmosphere of the little house, gave me a shock of hysterical fear and loathing. I could not touch it and I could not let it remain. I went into the scullery, got a bottle of ammonia and tipped it on to the earthworm. I do not know what prompted me to do this, unless my mother had given me an exaggerated idea of the corrosive powers of ammonia, because she did not want me to touch it. I thought that death would be instantaneous and it was not. The memory of this incident tortured me for many nights. It sickens me still.

Being superior we were allowed out less than most, but my happiest memories are of playing in the street and of our street companions. One of the pleasantest of these lived at the back of us, in Bride Street, and his name was "Jackie".

We were a cut above Bride Street and certainly the houses did look dirtier and poorer than those in Ellington Street. The only reason we were ever allowed to go into Bride Street was that there was a little group of shops there, including a sweetshop, a public house and a fish and chip shop. We never had fish and chips. It was probably too expensive.

On summer Sunday mornings, when the windows were open, there was always the sound of raucous singing and a clatter of cans and crockery from Bride Street and there was the sound of hens clucking and the crowing of a cock in someone's garden. Why the cock should have crowed only on Sunday is a mystery, since Friday seems more appropriate, but certainly these sounds are associated only with Sunday.

Jackie was younger than either of us and lived at the top of the house that backed on to ours. He used to look out of the window and call down to us, and, one day, he threw down one end of a long clothes-line. We tied a "message" on the end and he pulled it up again. This method of communication was difficult, because of the trees, and eventually he was allowed to come out to play with us.

Like most children round our way, we had a soap-box on wheels, which we called a "trolley". Even in this we were superior, for ours had been painted with the unattractive paint that my father had got for nothing. Jackie's mother liked him in pink and it did suit him. He had black bobbed hair cut with a fringe on his forehead, black, mischievous eyes, a round rosy face and a beautiful laughing red mouth out of which he spoke with a cockney accent so pronounced that even we, sometimes, could not understand him. He wore polished black shoes, little white socks and very short, pale pink trousers with a little belted pink tunic over them. By the time we sent him home everything about him was grey, and it was not long before he came out in some dark garments that had been roughly made out of some old ones of his father's. He was proud of these and we regarded them with approval.

All three of us would pile on to our trolley and go tearing down the hill. Nearly always Jackie was in tears, at least once, for he sat in front to steer and got the brunt of it when we hit the lamp-post or shot into the gutter. Always he laughed as the tears made tracks on his rosy cheeks. His nose ran and he never had a handkerchief. He liked playing with us.

One day a gipsy came to our door and I answered it. She was a very dark and frightening gipsy and wore gold ear-rings and a man's felt hat. We always said "No, thank you" to hawkers and they usually went away.

The gipsy was angry and insulting and I did not know the meaning of half the words she said, but I understood her last taunt, which she spoke with malicious gentleness, as she went down the steps: "Is father out of work, dear, that you can't afford it?"

Trembling, I asked her politely to shut the gate in order to keep the dogs out. She left it wide open and I was far too frightened to go down and shut it myself.

As I went back downstairs into the kitchen I knew that the gipsy had been right and wondered at her powers of divination. I had not known before, but I knew now; our father was one of the unemployed.

And many things which I had noticed out of the tail of my mind I now faced squarely; that my father always had time to walk half-way to school with me, that he would not tell me where he worked and that whenever he came home in the evening my mother said: "Any good?" as he entered the door, and he always shook his head. But he was never there when I came home to dinner. Where did they go, all these unemployed men, and what did they do all day, wandering about away from the house, so that the children should remain unaware of the family's plight? And mostly they had not even the price of a cup of tea in their pockets. The worst part of unemployment was the shame of it.

It was another child who pointed out to me that our mother was going to have a baby. I had often noticed it in other people's mothers and, I suppose, I had, in a way, known about my own, but the reality did not strike me and I did not seriously consider what it would be like to have a baby in the house.

A good deal of my time was spent in fantasy, much of which I shared with my brother. Usually I was not acutely conscious of a lack of material things, during the Ellington Street years, and yet all my fantasies, in one way or another, were concerned with at least a sufficiency if not a surfeit of such things.

There was a kind of picaresque serial story which I developed for my brother's benefit, each night, after we were in bed. The hero of these stories was a boy named "Bob Watson". The boy really existed. I used to see him at school, but knew him only by sight. I made of him a kind of juvenile Robin Hood. His hobby was doing good to the poor, but he did not have to steal in order to do it; he had everything at his disposal already, from sausage factories to knitting machines, and if, as the story went on, you should need, say, a pot of pepper, then he had ships that traded with the East and brought back sackfuls of the stuff. His favourite uncle was the very top head of the international police too, and he did exactly as Bob told him, so that any difficulties occasioned by Bob's own smallness and weakness were instantly met. It was almost too easy. But the story went on for months until it was superseded by something else.

This was not so much a story as the detailed description of a Utopia. It was a minute world, delicate and lovely and simply arranged. I first got the idea because of the little kangaroos. They were pin-head size and progressed by enormous leaps. I never actually saw anything else, in this world, only the little kangaroos and I never stopped to wonder why this should be

46

for, given these, I could, to my infinite delight, and my brother's, imagine all the rest. I dreamed all day at school.

A girl next to me in prayers said: "I wanted a dog but my mother won't let me. She says all animals have fleas."

I woke out of my imaginings and said: "No, my mother won't either."

It was not true, of course. I never thought now of asking for anything; I knew I should not be able to have it. The large world into which we fitted so precariously was always one of chance and lack, so that our joy in the small world was two-fold, for we rejoiced not only in its beauty but also in the abundance which arose from the smallness of its needs. In this was perfection.

It was the day of the school outing. Most of the others remembered a previous one, to Westminster, but I did not, as my school life had been shorter than theirs. Going to South Kensington, crossing the roads amidst all the traffic, jostling and piling on buses and the chaotic strangeness of it all made me feel that I had lost my identity and that, detached, I was looking down at myself amongst the other children, shepherded by rather self-conscious teachers. This feeling was the same as that which came in the nightmares, only less intense.

In the Natural History Museum, I hardly saw the giant water-lily, the stuffed gorilla nor even the baby elephant with wisps of thin hair on his head, but with a shock like the plunge of a hypodermic needle I saw the "thing".

"*Pulex irritans*", enlarged to about the size of my own head and varnished yellow, had spiny little hairs growing out of its lacquered scales. There was an obscene and complicated orifice up-ended near its tail, six legs with clawed toes and a grooved proboscis like a gouge. *Pulex irritans*; the realisation stabbed me. Such things were the little kangaroos. I read the information on the card beneath the glass; the Black Death; "bring out your dead"; carriers of plague. Later I was sick on the bus and they sent me home to bed, which was the last place on earth where I wanted to be.

I had a logical mind, but it was a subjective kind of logic and did not always accord with that of people around. For me, lights did not go out, they all came out, like stars, like flowers, like unfurled flags, and I was always causing confusion by saying that a light was out when I meant that it was shining. Also, the word "sweet" has a sharper sound than "sour", so that, in my earlier years, if I said that an orange was sweet, I meant that it was not. As I grew older and went to school, this kind of difficulty tended, in some ways, to increase. Being considered "clever" I several times missed a class and, consequently, part of the curriculum. Most of the gaps I could fill in for myself, but, in a few instances, the filling in was not entirely satisfactory.

I never could understand the parts of the verb "to be". The Verb To Be was like Kingdom Come. "In the beginning was the 'Word' " and in the end would be a word, but a particular, more specific word—in fact the Verb. This Verb was manifest in parts, although it was yet to be, and knowing those parts was like "seeing the light". It was a revelation which came to those who were good and obedient. Only to the approved, the competent and the self-sufficient was vouchsafed the joy of flinging up one's hand in class and singing out, eyes shining: "It's part of the verb 'to be'!" It was my continual prayer that I might one day have sufficient goodness and faith for such insight to be granted.

Before this wonderful thing could happen to me there came what I could only regard as the supreme and awful test. Suddenly, in class, our teacher said: "Write out the parts of the verb 'to be'!"

I did not know what to do, but everyone else was writing. I bit my pen and wrote also. This composition was not preserved, but I was greatly exercised over it and, to the best of my memory, it was this:

"Verb is Word and the beginning and the end are the same. In the beginning the Word and in the end the Verb To Be. It will come on the day of judgement. Parts of the Verb are here now and some people can tell them, but I am not good enough. I know this means that if Jesus came on earth again I would not know Him, either, and would be like the Scribes and the Pharisees. I have prayed and there is nothing else I can do."

My paper looked different from that of everyone else and I

slipped it under the pile. The crazy great butterfly swung about my head as we went out for drill in the playground.

When I received my paper again I found it was crossed through diagonally with two red lines, like weals, and in the corner was the scratchy command: "Come to me!"

I waited at play-time. The teacher had two coils of hair over her ears. She was tall and she stood on a dais.

"I've got something to say to you." She pointed to the paper. "Where did you get that?"

"I wrote it."

"Not out of your own head."

"Yes, I did."

"Show it to me again. I'm afraid I didn't read beyond the first two lines. I didn't think it was your own."

For a moment she looked at my writing, then she was standing half turned towards the window and her head seemed to be wobbling from side to side. She thrust the paper back at me and waved me away.

But at the end of the morning, I was summoned again.

"I asked you where you got that because it is very, very good. That is real writing. It is grown-up writing. Your English has always been good, but I did not think there was anyone in this school who could write like that."

I clutched my paper so that I crumpled it. I was so pleased that I forgot to smile. In all my life there had been only two other occasions when I had felt almost dizzy with delight; one was in the infants' school when I painted a Christmas card for a teacher and she kissed me, the other was at my first taste of a peach. It had been cut into four pieces for me and, when I had put the second piece into my mouth, out of pure joy, I squeezed the two remaining pieces till the juice dripped off my elbows.

Now I hardly knew what to do. I pushed the paper under my desk and went out of the room. Once in the street I ran and ran and ran. I could have run faster than anybody in the world. The thin scarlet cross on the paper had become a testimony, a token, and I no longer cared that I did not understand the parts of the verb "to be".

There had been a time, during my very young childhood, when I had refused to eat. In connection with this there was one incident that I particularly remember. It was on a picnic and I was given an enormous piece of cake which I eventually dropped. It rolled into some long grass and I was immediately praised for having eaten it. That would have been all right except that I performed such antics in order to ensure that it was properly hidden, that those in charge of me found it almost at once. Everybody laughed, but the feelings engendered in me were so strong that I broke into a desolate howl. I did not mind so much their knowing that I could not eat, I was often reproached for it. What really upset me was that they should know how I had been unable to acknowledge it, that they should see the measure of my shame. This I have always found difficult; to have to assert that I am not as white as I am painted.

I do not remember the transition from refusing food to wanting it passionately and being able to enjoy eating almost anything, but the latter condition obtained during most of my childhood.

There were three "scholarship classes", that is classes from which pupils were allowed to enter. Those in the lowest of these classes hardly ever got through and few succeeded from the second class. It was we, the *élite,* who attained the top class before entering, on whom the hopes of the school rested. This class was presided over by Mr. Chalk. That really was his name, and if he is alive now, he must be ninety at least. He was tall, cadaverous, pale and dry, but he once gave me a rose from his garden and I kept the petals in my pencil-box for years. By putting the class "on its honour" he could leave us all for as long as ten minutes without a word being spoken in his absence. No other teacher in the school could do this. There would be pandemonium in less than half the time. He was determined to instil into us a high standard of integrity and a knowledge of grammar.

One afternoon he spent teaching us the use of the verbs "to lie" and "to lay". Towards the end of this lesson he asked me whether I would say to a dog "Lay down!" or "Lie down!" I said: "Lay down!", which was true, and he asked me why. I knew by the way he asked that I was wrong, so I answered desperately: "Because you wouldn't speak correctly to a dog."

Chalky never laughed. His tissue-paper skin would have split

50

if he had, but, as he tottered back to his dais, he was seized by a kind of convulsive jerking, like the twitching of some creature that has met a violent death. His face was quite composed when he turned to us and the lesson proceeded without comment.

We were examined periodically by the school nurse, so there could not have been many fleas; and we were examined periodically by the school doctor, so, perhaps, there could not have been so very much wrong with Violet Leicester. The only remark the school nurse made about me was to say that I seemed to be "all clothes", which my mother accepted as a tribute to her good sense, but the doctor said of me that I was far too thin and that my posture was bad. My mother had to take me, each Friday, to St. Bartholomew's Hospital, at Smithfield, for remedial exercises and, for my thinness, I was ordered raw minced beef, if I would eat it, and a raw egg each day if I could be persuaded to swallow it. I would have taken either or both, without persuasion.

In the summer we went swimming at the public baths in Caledonian Road, the whole of our class, with a teacher in charge. For the first few times I loved the feel of being in the pool, but, as our swimming lessons progressed, it became obvious that something was wrong. After a few minutes of abandoning myself to the rock of the water, the whole of the bath began to tip. Even after I got out, the floor seemed to tilt madly and I could not stand up. This happened three times and then I was told that I must not go swimming any more. I did go, privately, on Saturday mornings, to the baths in Essex Road, with a group of other girls, and, very gradually and rather miserably, I learnt to swim a little, but, every time, I got the same sensation. Nobody thought it worth while to investigate this, until, in middle life, it was discovered that the balance in my middle ear did not adjust easily, and, with very little disturbance, I tended to fall about like a tumbler pigeon.

At school there were four of us who, by reason of our intelligence, were considered likely winners of scholarships, at eleven. For this reason we missed certain classes so that we should, as quickly as possible, reach a class where scholarship work was taught and we could spend one or two years at it. The names of the others were Titchy Gammon, Violet Leicester and Harry Gomm. We four became friends simply because, through our rapid promotion, we lost touch with other people of our age. Titch and I were the closest friends. Harry, being a boy, played in the other playground and Violet was odd. She was the gentlest creature I have ever met. She crept about like a bee that is woken in winter, and her hands and her voice were so soft as to be almost ineffectual. Even her legs were smooth, not mottled and sand-blasted like ours. Her hair was black and her face like parchment, with tiny threads of blood beneath the skin.

Harry was a fair, fresh-complexioned, matter-of-fact child, with an air of considering carefully everything he said. It was Harry who asked one of the teachers where babies came from. We all grinned and she smiled self-consciously and told him to ask his mother. He said he had done so, but she would not tell him. We all "knew", of course, but Harry was not the kind of person to be satisfied with any unsubstantiated rumour. Presumably he did eventually find someone to give him more information for it was he who told us about sexual intercourse. We were standing in Westbourne Road at the time. Violet said she did not believe it and closed her pale lips firmly. After a while she mentioned a bishop who had come to talk to us at Sunday school. We all remembered him.

Violet whispered: "He's got a daughter, hasn't he? Well, do you mean to say that he did?"

Harry hesitated, obviously shaken in his conviction. But I knew that he had been right. It fitted so perfectly with adult jokes that I had overheard and with my own vague sensations. I felt that this would be the logical culmination of them. Besides, I did not have Violet's faith in the behaviour of adults. But when I tried to argue, I found that I had no words in which to say what I meant. And, suddenly, Titch turned on Harry, her eyes bright with tears and her tiny figure trembling. She slapped his face, so that he staggered, and then ran away. She sped towards Sonning Street, where she lived, running with quick, nervous movements of her matchstick arms and legs and jerkily, like the motion pictures we infrequently saw. At any other time we would have run after Titch and started a fight, yet, now, we knew that, for some reason, she was beside herself and, by tacit consent, neither Harry nor I did anything about it. Dear Harry, with his honesty and his innocence, was up against more than he knew.

For some time I had known, also, about menstruation, but discussed this only with older girls. I was very tall and, at school, in a high class for my age. I think that many of my acquaintances did not realise that I was only nine years old. By the time I was nearly eleven some of the girls I knew had turned fourteen and had left school. I still met them in the street in the evenings. They carried handbags and wore light stockings and high-heeled shoes. Their skirts were short, nearly up to their knees and, most exciting of all, they wore long silk knickers and fancy garters. (These are an aspect of the fashions of the twenties to which the recent revival has failed to do justice.) Sometimes my brother and I would imitate these girls who, when they ran, wrapped their skirts round them, tightly, clamped their knees together and kicked their heels sideways, but, in some ways, I wanted to be like them.

I was often in fights, but only one is memorable, and that is the one I had with Flossy Bray. She lived along our street and her father was a bus-conductor. The first thing I remember about her is that she was absent from school when I was promoted to the class in which we became acquainted. She had had scarlet fever and, when she came back, everyone crowded round her. My mother said I should keep away, because I might still catch it. In spite of this she and I became sufficiently friendly for me to lie about my age, so that I should be put in her class at Sunday school. She had an umbrella and we used to drop our "collection" halfpennies into it, so that we could buy sweets with them later.

She was ten and I was only eight. I still say she started it, by pushing me against a lamp-post which had just been painted a vivid moss green. The lamp-post was not merely sticky, it was quite wet and the palms of my hands were as green as though they belonged to a giant frog, after I had grasped it to prevent myself falling into the gutter. Flossy laughed, but came too near, so that I pushed one hand into her face. Then she wiped her own hands round the lamp-post and slapped me. We began slapping each other as fast as we could, getting fresh supplies of paint at intervals. We moved down the street. There were more lamp-posts and more paint. Soon the lower parts of most of the lamp-posts were almost denuded. Flossie looked spectral and macabre and there was paint on her brand-new panama hat. I found a handkerchief and wiped my face, which probably smeared it a little. Then Flossie and I went home, separately.

The looks of people I met should have told me that I would not get away with it, although I tried to walk into the house as though nothing had happened, except that I was a little late.

While my father was cleaning me with turpentine, my mother wrote a note to Flossie's mother to say that Flossie and I were not to play together any more. As I ran down the street to put the note in their letter-box I passed a turpentine-washed Flossie, running up it, to put a note in ours. I had the advantage and beat her by two houses and the top step, but I suppose they won, since Flossie's mother had written her note in the third person.

After we went to live in Ellington Street we used to go home by way of Thornhill Road and Westbourne Road. I must have been late on one particular evening because I met Boyce's daughter, who had been to fetch a barrow, which she was taking home. Her father was a greengrocer and pushed a barrow through our streets each day, while he shouted his wares. Quite a number of people did this. A winkle-man came round on Sundays at tea-time, so did the muffin-man. He rang a bell and carried the muffins in a tray on his head. I always associated him with the lamp-lighter who carried a long pole, with which he lit the gas lamps in the streets. There was a rag and bone man, to whom we sold jam-jars, and even the coal-man, riding on top of his cart, called out "Coal".

What the greengrocer, Boyce, was supposed to be calling, we did not know, although we used to imitate him. It was one of those peculiarly cockney cries in which some complicated phrase is reduced to a single extraordinary monosyllable.

I do not remember the name of Boyce's daughter, but she was a friend of mine, and when I saw her pushing the barrow I offered to help. I enjoyed walking in the road in order to do this. While we were pushing, two people came along from opposite directions; one was my father, coming to meet me, and the other was one of our schoolmasters.

This schoolmaster was extremely unpopular. He had a son and a daughter, both of whom he brought to attend the school in which he taught. Very early, he kept them with him in his own class, although they were far too young. They were extremely unpopular, too. He was a rather small man with the kind of smooth good looks which my father disliked.

The schoolmaster smiled, in a social way, and said: "Your daughter?"

My father was furious. I could see the fury pulling at his lips behind his moustache and dragging at the pouches under his eyes. The schoolmaster walked on. My father told me to leave the barrow and go home, by myself, the other way. He spent the whole of that evening telling me, in little bursts of anger, how coarse and common I had looked, pushing a coster barrow along the road.

The effect of all this was rather spoilt when Boyce's girl, giggling, in school next day, told me that my father had pushed the barrow home for her himself, while she walked on the pavement.

# CHAPTER IV

## *BETTER THAN DOLLS*

MY brother and I took many walks of exploration by the method which, so early in life, had taken me to the police station. As I grew older, I passed the police station without noticing it. On these walks, I first became conscious of the fact that surroundings can be beautiful. Highbury New Park was one of the places I discovered. It seemed to me to be the height of social attainment to live there. I felt slightly elevated through merely walking along it, as though I did this every day of my life.

For sheer poetic beauty there was the New River where it comes out in Canonbury. I thought it was a canal, for it seemed, even to me, to have the look of a drab commercial waterway. I loved it all the same, and went there often, just to stand on Willow Bridge and look at it, stretched flatly between the man-made embankments, the skin of it rucked by the wind, deliciously.

Near here, somewhere, in a cul-de-sac, I found my perfect house. Like a dream house, it was there only once. I was never able to find it again. It was a small house, built of clean-looking red brick, the woodwork was painted a fresh, dark green and it had the kind of door-step on which nobody trod. There was a tiny, close-clipped lawn in the front garden, like a green baize table-cloth, and the window-boxes and the minute garden borders were neat and brilliant with geranium, coreopsis, lobelia and alyssum.

All of these things belonged to a different life, one to which I might eventually aspire, provided I went the right way about it. There was only one way; I must work hard and get a scholarship. After that I might work in an office, perhaps even the Civil Service, like my uncle, and then all things would be open to me.

We four, Violet, Titch, Harry and I were the ones most likely to get scholarships, but it was also likely that one or two of us would fail, because it was so rare for more than two scholarships to be won from the same school. It was only a question of English and arithmetic, and we scholarship children hardly did anything else. English I did not worry about. My arithmetic was good, but it needed the added stimulus of an examination to make it so. For most of the term I was at the bottom of the form, and only after the end-of-term tests did I find myself near the top.

But how we worked! My mother coached me at home, in arithmetic, and sent notes to school to ask if I might do extra sums during needlework, during painting, during games. This last did not bother me, for I had come to loathe games. Titch was so small and Violet so slow that nobody expected anything of them, but I was as big as anyone in the class. Everybody, including I, seemed to forget that I was at least two years younger than most of them and that, in spite of my size, my physical attainments were likely to be less than theirs.

In these things the only time when I felt anything but hopeless was during the annual sports. The whole school took part and we were classified strictly according to age. I would suddenly find myself set to run against people whom I had long regarded as small fry; I could run like a hare and always came in first, but this occurred only once a year.

Soon I came to realise that there was something wrong with my mother. She took to going to bed before we did and I would carry up her supper of bread and cheese, tomatoes and cocoa. I did not question this, but just accepted that she was not well. Then, one day, at about seven in the morning, my father came in to wake me and to say that my mother was ill and I must fetch Dr. Ambrose as soon as I was dressed and without waiting for any tea.

I had long hair which, at night, was tied up in little bits of tape, not because it needed curling, but because it got into such a complicated tangle. I could not stop to undo them, but stuffed these little bundles of hair into a huge tam-o'-shanter which had been my mother's before she was married. It was a brilliant dandelion yellow. As my mother had run along Arundel Square, at the sound of my screaming, so I ran up it from Ellington Street, frightened out of my wits by her groans. I whipped along Offord Road and the Liverpool Road. I do not remember going back again, and perhaps I did not do so, for my father's sister, "Auntie Soo", lived in Arundel Square, and we went there for our midday meal.

At school I told our teacher that my mother had pneumonia. It was the only serious, non-infectious illness that I knew of. I wondered why she smiled.

I do not know what time of day it was that my brother and I were allowed to see our mother. We were ushered in by a coarse, elderly woman with a lot of white hair, who, I was told, was the nurse. She was not my idea of a nurse, but I forgot her as soon as I went in. I forgot my mother too. There, on the near side of the double bed, was an iron cot and, in it, on the white pillow, two little puce-coloured faces; not one, but two.

I did not like dolls, but I liked these. My brother said: "Are they ours?" And they were. In fact, they were mostly mine. I was a girl and nearly ten. I could look after them easily. But my brother said quickly, as he always did: "One each", and my mother agreed. Then the nurse picked up a baby by the front of its gown in just one of her great hands and I wanted to hit her. I would not have allowed even one of my despised dolls to be picked up like that.

I went away and wrote down the date of the birth of my sisters in a notebook. It was so terribly important, and I felt that if I did not do this it might be forgotten.

Quite soon I became what was called "very good with the babies". My mother believed in their being wheeled out every day for two hours in "any weather except fog or an east wind". We rarely had either. I was allowed to choose when I should do this, morning or afternoon. During the other half of the day I worked for my scholarship.

When I first took the babies out everyone crowded round to look, but I said they must not do this because of germs, and they went away. I did not mind. I was far prouder of the pram I was pushing than of any of my inadequate skills at games. Occasionally I watched my friends throwing their balls against the smooth wall of Mr. More's the chemist, but I had been told never to let go of the pram and I soon became tired of standing and walked up and down again.

My mother's sister had twins too, but they were only a boy and a girl, not identical twin girls like ours, nevertheless, many of their clothes were passed down to us and so was their first perambulator. This was a massive thing, tall as a tram and as unwieldy. When the shades were up the babies were almost completely enclosed in a sort of tent. This they enjoyed when they became old enough to notice it, but the shades had the disadvantage of making it quite impossible for me to see where we were going. In crossing the road this became quite dangerous, not so much because of the traffic as because it was necessary to get the pram at right angles to the kerb. The pram was so ill-balanced that it would tip over sideways if either wheel were lowered before the other. Once I misjudged this and, to my horror, felt the pram getting out of control. I was not strong enough to pull it back; I could not prevent it falling over if I pushed it on. I could do nothing but cling to it, throwing on all my weight, and look up and down the cruelly deserted street. Then, a long way down the road I saw Ralph Roberts's father. He and I had hated each other for years. He had a violent temper and aggressively bulging dark brown eyes. He worked at night, and tried to sleep during the day, while we rattled sticks on his railings and ran our thunderous trolley past his house.

He shouted at me now. How well I knew that furious voice. How often had I seen him run, as he was doing now. How often had I jeered and widened the distance between him and me. Now I could not move, but I began to build the blackest of all dark curses against him should he cause me to upset the babies.

As soon as he reached me he seized the pram, hoisted it on to the pavement, then pushed it down the kerb for me. I would not let him have the pram, but hung on, shaken about like a rag doll. Then, to my surprise, he just stood on the pavement and wiped his forehead under his cap. I got to the other side of the road and then looked back at him, and I was nearly in tears with gratitude, not so much at what he had done but because he could do it for an enemy. I vowed then that if I ever again had the chance to rattle a stick on his railings or to play "knocking down ginger" on his door so as to watch him come out, I would refrain. I do not know whether I could have kept that vow or not.

There was one other person whose high moral tone impressed me and that was Donald Soper, then at the new Islington Central Hall. He ran a twopenny cinema for children. We hardly ever went to the "pictures", although many of our friends did, but we saw *The Kid* with our mother, and sat through it, with tears streaming down our faces and boiled sweets in our mouths. One felt very good and exalted afterwards. My father took us to see Harold Lloyd in *Speedy*. But, for a time, we did go regularly to the Central Hall, for one of the films shown was a serial, which we could not miss. On the occasion which I remember so well the supporting film was suddenly switched off and Donald Soper came on to the stage to address us. He said that he had only just realised that the film was unsuitable and we must all go home. We were a rough lot and many were much older and bigger than my brother and I. There must have been several hundreds of us and we could not have our money back, but we went and nobody seemed to mind very much having had a moral lecture instead of the show we had come for. I remembered this when, years later, I saw Soper pulled from a wall on Tower Hill where he was preaching pacifism during the war.

I enjoyed the films, once they began; what I did not like was the feeling of being herded together in a vast crowd. There was the same feeling at the party given by the Lord Mayor for children of the unemployed.

Whenever I was not improving my arithmetic or minding the babies I was reading. My concentration was as impenetrable as the jelly round frog's spawn. I read anything. I could never get enough books. For months I begged my mother to let me join the public library. She said there would be bugs in the books. There were, but only dead ones, "mahogany flats" pressed between the pages.

In Ellington Street we had a large basement kitchen. A door led from it into the coal-cellar where I used to sit, sometimes, pretending it was a cave. Beside the cellar door were double doors which led into the area. These were hardly ever opened, because, in front of them, the babies slept during the day.

For a long time we called them "the big one" and "the little one". This was because, when they were born, one had weighed seven pounds and the other, the elder, only five and a half. For this reason the little one became "mine" while my mother would always carry the big one. It was supposed to be because the little one would be easier for me to manage, but, in fact, after the first few weeks, the little one caught up and there were times when the little one was bigger than the big one, by two or three ounces, but the names stuck and the little one remained mine.

Immediately in front of the area doors were two pieces of furniture which were acquired, I think, at the birth of my twin sisters. First was an ancient sofa. I do not remember any-one ever sitting on it. A long wicker basket cradle was placed there in which the little one lay during the day. Beside the sofa was a large chair. This had two flat wooden arms with grooves to take a stick, which supported the back of the chair. The stick had been removed altogether and the back let down to rest on a stool, thus making a long flat bed for the big one.

At one end of this kitchen was a large dresser and a vast amount of paraphernalia was kept on it, in it or under it. The lower part was curtained off and, here, there seemed to be all the boots and shoes of past centuries. Whenever we changed our shoes for the slippers we wore in the house, we threw them under there, and finding them again was sometimes a major work of excavation, rummaging in the dark amongst old high-heeled, buttoned boots which my mother had, for years, thought too good to throw away.

At the other end of the kitchen was another cooking-range, bigger and blacker than the one in Arundel Square. There was one period during which my brother and I used to light the kitchen fire in the mornings. This was because my father had been directed to some work which was outside London and necessitated his living away, although he came home at week-ends, bearing bunches of country flowers. Many of the un-employed were "organised" in this way.

We always felt very proud of our fire, and throughout the

day would look at it and remark that we had started it. Once we started more than we meant to, setting fire to some washing which had been hung over the fireplace to air. I was in the coal-cellar, heard my brother cry out, and came in to see him swinging a long pair of pants at the fire with the intention of beating it out.

There was a watering-can on the hearth so that we could replenish kettles without going into the scullery, and I poured the water from this over the flames.

Another time a deep-fat frying-pan caught fire. It was dreadful and uncontrollable. My brother ran through the cellar door, I picked up the babies, banging their heads together, and my mother picked up the pan; she wrapped a rug round it, carried it out and flung the flaming thing into the garden. (I have since seen a whole cottage destroyed because its owner could not act as quickly as my mother did then.)

Very much part of our family were the cats. There was always a cat. I can remember twenty-one cats, over the years, and only one of them is worth a second thought. We called him "Big Ginger", and he was the ugliest and most vicious brute this side of the bars. He was a "stray", a haunter of roof gutters and a knocker-off of dustbin lids. My mother fed him once, out of pity, and then spent weeks trying to persuade herself that he was "all right really". His coarse coat was dung-dust-coloured and he had two eyes, but it was a moot point whether or not he could see out of both of them. What was left of his ears looked like chewed cardboard. Nobody ever nursed him or spoke cat-talk to him. He would have spat in your eye if you had, for he himself was articulate and spoke with an atrocious cockney accent, making just those twisted complicated vowel sounds that the street criers reiterated. All London cats use cockney in this way, but none with so large a vocabulary and so little euphony as did Big Ginger.

We were all half afraid of him, and my father said that if Big Ginger even so much as hissed at the babies the brute would have his neck wrung. Yet, although my brother and I touched him at our peril and he frequently shed our blood, for months he refrained from doing anything that would merit his own destruction.

The babies were very small, only just able to walk, when the most alarming incident occurred. One of my tiny sisters came stumbling into the room almost entirely submerged in cat. Her soft little arms were bare and hugging Big Ginger round the middle of his horrible body, a dirty-looking paw rested on each of her little shoulders and his battered, lecherous old face lay against her neck; they were angelic, blue-eyed babies. Between her little padding feet, his great tail trailed. His hind paws only just cleared the ground. In front of the fire she let him go and he slipped to the floor like the yolk of some dirty great egg.

When really small the babies could pull him about, tugging at ears and tail and seizing handfuls of fur. Big Ginger would sit hunched up, his scarred face screwed tight with malice, and regard them out of the slits of his nasty-looking eyes. They wrapped him up in shawls.

For all of this they paid the penalty later on. He seemed to know exactly at what age he could begin to tyrannise, and by the time they were three or four they did not dare to pass him if he sat on the dark and narrow basement stairs.

Then, one day, my sisters, standing at the window of my parents' bedroom, called to me gleefully to come and look, and there was Big Ginger running along the tops of the walls, between the gardens. We thought at first that he had a rat, until a woman, down Bride Street, started shrieking that it was one of her kittens.

My father, who was very agile, went out, leapt on to the wall and began chasing Big Ginger, shouting at him in Hindustani, and Big Ginger deposited the kitten on the wall and himself fled. All the Bride Street windows were flung up as my father, seething, carried back the kitten. His anger was really at the fact that he had lost his slipper and had a hole in his sock.

For days we were insufferably funny about "kidnapping" and "cat-napping", and my mother left a window open for Big Ginger, who slunk back at night to crouch under the dresser with the boots and shoes.

But Ginger could not curb his philoprogenitive instincts and the Bride Street woman said that they were valuable kittens and she would call the police and we should be fined if we could not control our cat. It was too much. Ginger had to go.

There seem now to be so many organisations that can help poor people over their animals that I cannot understand why my father decided to manage this himself. We were not supposed to know, but we did, and stood with our noses pressed against the glass of the scullery door as soon as our father became absorbed in what he was doing. I used to think that, whenever my father was angry or nervously tense for any other reason, that the scar on his lip turned white and showed through his moustache. He looked like that now.

First he took the bucket from under the stone sink, threw the floor-cloths out of it and began to fill the copper. He made it so full that water swelled gently over the edge. Ginger lay waiting, resting his chin on the stone floor and making slits of his eyes. My father swore under his breath, picked up Ginger by the scruff and the hind legs, plunged him in and jammed the heavy wooden lid on top. Water slopped over the edge of the copper and on to my father's feet. There had been no struggle.

My father leaned on the copper lid with one hand and straightened his moustache with the other. Suddenly there was a crash. The lid flew up and a ginger streak shot out, trailing water, as a comet trails sparks. The scullery window had been closed; now it was open, swinging on weak hinges, while my father stood with a scratch the length of his forearm and blood, in a beaded fringe, running from it. My brother went into one of his fits of silent laughter. In fact we all of us laughed ourselves sick. My father put salt on his wound, which he always did, to disinfect and stop the bleeding, and my mother smiled when she came in and heard of it all, for she too was relieved. We did not see Ginger again and he was the only cat I could ever have loved.

My brother and I slept in a room at the back of the kitchen and next to the scullery. There were double doors giving on to the garden from here, but they were never opened. My bed was next to the window, and at the end of it and against the wall was the large mahogany chest of drawers. The two small top drawers were always locked, the drawer below this was mine, and the one below that my brother's and the bottom drawer was the one in which my mother had found the sheeting for Alby (but after the babies were born, I forgot Alby and do not even know what happened to him). To the left of the chest of

64

drawers was another black cooking-range, for our bedroom had once been a kitchen. Apart from the coal cellar and the lavatory, this range was the most fascinating place in the whole house. It was concealed by a purple curtain which added to its mystery. The stove was all rusted and full of soot and broken brick. You could climb on top of it and huddle in the chimney piece. The oven was a repository for our darkest, deepest, secret treasures and everything, not in this world, was up the chimney.

In the wall facing the window was a cupboard. This was quite an interesting place, too. One could stand in it, and on either side were shelves going very far back. My mother stored linen on these shelves, and the linen must, one day, have been somewhat diminished, for at the back of it I noticed what I had never seen there before—books. I brought them all out, two or three hundred of them and all kinds, from a slim *Don Juan* to a thick *Dr. Johnson*. A few of these I had read in the public library. Most of them I had not read at all. I asked my father about them. He said they were his and suddenly became enthusiastic and I discovered that my semi-literate father, who could hardly write well enough to fill in a crossword puzzle, had a passion for books and, in particular, the poetry of Byron.

He did not like Shakespeare and did not read any, but he had read for pleasure such authors as Scott, Dickens, Thackeray and Macaulay as well as Dumas and Stanley Weyman. Quite casually, when I could get out of doing arithmetic, I absorbed most of these and told my brother about the last two. Once or twice I tried to read to him, but this was not successful, and he decided that I could make the stories of Dumas far more interesting than could Dumas himself.

For the scholarship exam we went to Thornhill Road and sat in the large strange hall, in the strange school. I was glad that one of our teachers was there and that it was the one who had liked my writing. My mother had assured me and everyone else that I was not nervous, so I assumed that my feeling of fear and reluctance must be something different.

If I did not get through the scholarship I should have to work in a factory. Sometimes, going home with my mother, after dark, on a Saturday night, I would see girls of fourteen or fifteen sauntering along, eating chips from greasy newspaper. They were always laughing loudly and shouting and pushing each other off the kerb. I was frightened of them and my mother said that they were factory girls and, if I did not get a scholarship, then I should become like them and have similar people as my constant companions. It did not occur to me that they were not all the same, that some of my friends left school and went into factories with no great change of manner. I knew somebody who twisted sausages and another who stitched overalls. I did not want to do either of these things.

Rene was already at the high school to which I hoped to go. Things had not been so disastrous for her parents as they had for mine, and they were able to pay for her to go to a private school and then as a fee-paying pupil to Highbury.

At school I now moved out of the scholarship class and into a higher one. I stopped doing arithmetic in my spare time. I painted a picture of two apples on a plate and sewed some meat-cloth overalls for the babies. Mostly I sat reading.

When I realised, after school prayers one morning, that we were now going to be given the scholarship results, everything became blurred. Violet was called out to the front of the hall and a wave of clapping rose that made my head swim. I started to clap, like everyone else, but in a kind of hysteria. The headmaster called Titch, then Harry.

When he said: "Three. I think that's very good, don't you?" I knew I hadn't got it, and I wondered what it would be like going home that dinner-time to say that I had failed. I wondered whether or not I should be able to say anything about it at all, and thought of the days of torment while I kept it to myself. I thought of seeing Titch and Violet and Rene going to the High School while, for three more years, I went backwards and forwards to Barnsbury Park.

The headmaster was speaking again and I hardly heard what he said: "Just a minute, there's one more."

The voice went on, but it was not my name. Somebody poked me in the back. Somebody said: "Go on! You!"

Seconds after the headmaster had spoken the meaning of his words broke through. I must have put my names in the wrong order on the entrance form and he had read them out that way.

66

I was pushed along the row from hand to hand but I walked to the front by myself. I stood with the other three beside the headmaster's desk and the clapping sounded like a shower of stones against a wall. Very slowly the corner of the desk came towards me. I held it with one hand and it remained still. Two teachers who had started forward went back again.

In the classroom somebody said: "Look, her face is green."

"It's really pale green. Look."

Everybody pushed to look at my green face. Their voices sounded a long way away and I could not say anything. I felt that, if I spoke, nobody would be able to hear me. The teacher came in and we four were allowed to run home then, in the strange middle-of-school hours, to tell our parents.

During the school holidays I would go with my mother to the child welfare clinic on Friday afternoons. Here the babies were weighed and seen by the doctor. It was convenient for my mother to have me. All the mothers sat in the warm room which was decorated with print screens. Here we undressed our babies and wrapped them in their shawls. Sometimes we had to stand with the babies in our arms for what seemed to me to be a very long time. My baby, the little one, would grow heavier and heavier. Sometimes she started to slip and the shawl would slip in a different direction. The little one must have felt decidedly insecure at times. Bits of baby would come out of the shawl at inappropriate places. Then somebody would laugh, take my baby, wrap it up again and give it back to me. I resented this.

After I started at the High School I was still able to go to the welfare clinic with my mother because, at this school, Friday was a half-day. I enjoyed sitting around with the mothers, listening to the stories of their confinements and discussing the weights of the babies. But the proudest times of my life were the hours that I spent wheeling the pram up and down the street and wearing my new school hat. Old ladies who lived along the better side of Arundel Square used to stop me and say what a good girl I was to look after the babies and what a clever girl to have got a scholarship. I never wanted to do anything except walk up and down.

It took me fifteen minutes to go from Ellington Street to

Highbury Hill High School. There was a bus that ran along Liverpool Road, Drayton Park and Highbury Hill but I never used it. We did not even think of my using it. Instead I walked through the church gardens, Fieldway Crescent, Highbury Crescent, the terrace and into the back entrance of the school. At midday I had half an hour in which to eat my lunch at home before I walked back again.

In nineteen twenty-eight, the year in which my sisters were born, our school building had been built. Before that the school had occupied three houses, one on the present site of the school and two opposite. Rene could remember the school in these houses and so could Sonia.

I had noticed her often at prayers. She liked to be noticed. She was "best friends" with a girl named Marjorie Larner and they were often to be seen giggling together. Sonia was remarkable mostly for her extremely low and resonant voice and her precise diction. She had tremendous vitality. For her, life was all drama and excitement. When it was not she made it so. She had a swarthy skin with a glow under it and enormous eyes like pigeons' eggs. Her teeth were large and white in a large, frog-wide mouth and the mouse-brown of her rather coarse, nearly straight hair was grained with gold.

One day we found ourselves together at netball. She was shooter and I was goal defence. The game was at the other end of the court. Sonia was not much interested in it and I had not played ball for months. I could never now work up any enthusiasm for games. If another person wanted the ball they were welcome to it. I had other things to think about.

Sonia told me that her mother was a professional 'cellist. I did not even know what a 'cello was. Sonia's father had been killed in the war and her mother had, fairly recently, married someone whom Sonia called "Pops" and who worked in a bank. They lived in Hendon, some distance away, and Sonia had the distinction of travelling to school by Underground. One way and another she had quite a lot of distinction.

Suddenly there was a shout from the games mistress. The ball made an arc over the pitch and began to descend towards my head. I should have leapt at it eagerly, received it in stinging palms and sent it sailing towards the other goal. Instead I ducked. The ball bounced on the backs of my hands, with which I had covered my head, and then went rolling away over one of the white lines.

Walking home that evening, along Highbury Terrace, I heard Sonia and Marjorie behind me. I turned and waited until they caught up and we all three went on together. We left Marjorie in Fieldway Crescent. This was not the most direct route to Holloway Road Station, where Sonia was going, but it was the way they always went. After Marjorie had left us I continued with Sonia to the station. This became a habit, also; we talked for longer each evening and I began to get home very late. One day Sonia asked me to tea.

This was something almost unheard of by my family. People simply did not go to tea with one another. One talked to neighbours, children played in the street with their friends, and that was that. Sometimes in the past, in Arundel Square, some cousins would come to spend Sunday with us or we would go to them, but we had somehow ceased to do this once we moved to Ellington Street. Further, Sonia lived a long way away. It necessitated getting a train to King's Cross, another to Golders Green and a bus from there to the Great North Way. It meant my coming back alone. And there was the fare.

Sonia had far more pocket money than I and offered, very nicely, to pay this. My parents were shocked. We were poor, but we had our standards, so at last, after much argument and leaving the address and the telephone number with my mother, I went.

The house in which Sonia lived in Holders Hill Avenue was, I suppose, quite ordinary and suburban but the atmosphere was more affluent and more cultured than any I had known. The house smelt of new soft furnishings, coffee, floor polish and fruit. Our house did not smell of any of these things. There were books and not just the recognised classics that I had found at home, but modern books which were as difficult to read and presumably as "good" as anything I had, so far, looked into. In the dining-room was a polished table of dark oak, which was set with little mats. It was vastly different from the kitchen table at home, with its oil-cloth and its "picked" corners. In the drawing-room were two 'cellos and a beautiful piano. They had a bathroom too and Sonia had a tiny bedroom of her own where we sat and talked until supper-time.

It was obvious at once that Sonia's mother did not approve of me. Sonia and I had anticipated this and decided to say that I could help her with her arithmetic homework. It was true, and was, moreover, instantly accepted, and I discovered gradually that prowess in this subject was a passport into the homes of almost any of the girls I met at the High school.

Sonia's maternal grandmother lived with them. She had the same attractive voice and precise diction that I had admired in Sonia. Apart from this, I remember her in connection with only one other incident.

Sonia and I both disliked gym. To enjoy it one needs to be something of an exhibitionist, which was not possible for me, once my first school uniform began to wear out. I was supposed to do my own mending because my mother was so busy, but I doubt if the most expert needlewoman could have kept me looking presentable with the time and the materials which were available to me. My black, woollen stockings were always too short, and conspicuous ladders used to spring from the suspenders. I used to "ink them over", so that they showed less, and carefully fit the ladders on to the ink each morning. If it had not been for the stockings I think I should at least have liked climbing ropes because of the romantic associations. Sonia too, liked climbing ropes, but her associations were different.

Having climbed, we were supposed to come down hand over hand, the only parts of our bodies in contact with the rope being our hands, our feet and our knees. This did not always happen as planned and Sonia, coming down, experienced a sensation which she found suddenly and alarmingly pleasurable. She told me about it but I did not understand. I was more than a year younger than she and, in any case, I never did use things like ropes. I had similar feelings as a very young child and in play at Barnsbury Park, although nothing of the intensity that Sonia described. But I accepted Sonia's need for a rope quite easily, as it was no more strange than many other things I had begun to accept since I had known her. Between us we resolved that she must have some of her own.

Sonia told her grandmother that this was necessary and I confirmed it. Everyone at school had rope, I said, the thick kind that we used in the gym. I had some myself, even I. It was one of those things that were absolutely essential if one were to take part in the social life of the school. And Sonia stood there, like a child in an advertisement, pathetic, inferior, frustrated and deprived for lack of this piece of rope. Her grandmother's heart was touched.

It was arranged that we should make an expedition on the following Saturday morning to a shop in the Seven Sisters Road. This shop sold nothing but rope, from finest "T" twine to cables as thick as your arm. The shop assistant was a brusque and efficient man. He listened carefully to Sonia's description and then asked what she wanted it for. We said skipping. He was incredulous. How could we skip with rope an inch in diameter? He told us to feel the weight of it. Then he told us the price of it. We were not able to play on his emotions as we had done on Grandma's. Slowly and methodically he undid all that I had done to influence her and finally pointed out that skipping with a rope as thick as that would be dangerous. In the end we bought a length of clothes-line, which for Sonia, was no use at all. Our failure depressed me, because Grandma was so earnest. She underlined words in the Victorian manner and she had been so anxious that the child should have the Right Kind of rope.

# CHAPTER V

## *NEW VISTAS*

MY ability in arithmetic took me into the homes of several of the girls at school, but Sonia was the only one of these who was ever allowed to come home with me. The attitude of Sonia's mother was a permissive one, largely because she was too much occupied with her music for it to be anything else. Sonia took to coming, without any prearrangement, and sat with us at our kitchen table and ate large slices of our thick, soft-crusted white bread. We began to spend more and more of our time together, sitting, usually, in a room by ourselves, to talk. This arrangement was accepted by both families and indirectly, through us, they got to know each other, although, I think, our mothers met only once.

I remember Sonia's mother remarking to me that my mother must be very busy with her babies just as she herself was busy with her concerts. I do not know whether or not my scorn showed in my face. I think it must have done, especially as Sonia had told me how years ago her mother had been wont to cry at their poverty and say that she would have to play the 'cello in the streets. She and Sonia had then lived mainly on unearned in-come that was more than my father now had for six of us.

My parents were impressed by my tales of Sonia's home (which I exaggerated more and more) and Sonia's mother was impressed by our contrivances. She got the idea of making a coat for Sonia.

The school coat that I wore was a beautiful affair. It was made of the finest serge and almost entirely covered with an intricate arrangement of tiny tucks. It had been given to us by my cousin's grandmother. It was a real period piece, dating, I should say, from about the end of the war. As my mother told me, it was a lovely bit of material.

When Sonia first came in her coat she said at once that she

hated it. I glanced at it with a fairly experienced eye. The collar was all right, the lapels sat quite well and the buttonholes were not bad, but with a tremor I realised what was wrong. The sleeves had been set in the wrong armholes so that they curved gently backwards. I mentioned this to Sonia and she looked annoyed. I began to titter. I had suffered so much over my own coat that I could not help it. In the end I laughed outright. I laughed in a way that I had not done since the beginning of adolescence. It was nearly the end of a friendship that proved, for Sonia, to be life-long.

From Arundel Square we had gone on holiday, as a family. When I won a scholarship I was invited to stay with various relatives for a week each, to help me recover from the strain. My brother failed to win a scholarship to a high school, only to Barnsbury Park Central School, so, in the matter of holidays, he was not privileged as I was. My mother and my sisters had stayed at St. Leonards-on-Sea through a charitable organisation which was concerned with the relief of the unemployed. They had some form of service and sang a hymn morning and evening. The happiest holiday that I had with a member of my own family was the one I spent with my brother in the Cambridgeshire Fens.

Mr. and Mrs. Butcher lived in Rose Cottage. They were old now. My father had known them and stayed with them years before I was born. That summer must have been glorious for I cannot remember staying indoors at all, but I remember the lit marsh gas at night over the fen and the wall-high sedge that grew all over the marsh. There were water-lilies on the Lode, which flooded in winter and forget-me-nots grew wild all along its edge. I made wreaths of these with the village girls and we wore them in our hair. We constructed boats which sank in the weed-thick water and spent hours high up amongst the leaves of willows. Sometimes we went beetle-hunting with people from the university, who took photographs of me, barefoot and flower bedecked. Once we went by horse-drawn barge to Upware. I remember the blousy women, from the cottages, sitting in the boat, their big print bosoms swelling above their aprons and their serge skirts, and their large hats riding like upturned corracles. It thundered wickedly on the return journey and I huddled warm beneath a tarpaulin, amongst the polished black boots.

One of the worst aspects of unemployment, for my father, was that he was intensely patriotic. He had fought with genuine idealism in the Boer War, the Indian frontier wars and the Great War. In the last, he was seriously wounded. Later, he was often conscious of this old wound and my mother tried to persuade him to apply for a pension. This he refused to do until it was too late. He said that he would always be able to earn enough to keep his wife and family. Perhaps it was for this and not for the jonquils that my mother could never forgive him. Afterwards, to be called an "idler", and "parasite", as the unemployed were, at this time, must have been very bitter. How deeply the insecurity affected my mother I did not appreciate for some while.

One Saturday there was a wedding in our street, at a house on the opposite side of the road. We stood on our top step to watch, and so did the people upstairs, and my father, who had just come home. When the bride appeared, somebody called my mother who was in the basement, and she came running up, but nobody from our house saw the bride, for my mother dropped unconscious in the hall. My father had been sitting sideways on the railings, swinging one leg. My mother got the sudden impression that he was being supported by the people around him. She told me afterwards that her constant fear was that my father might one day collapse from his old wound and then be totally disabled with no pension.

In the early thirties things seem to have deteriorated generally. My sisters knew children who went to school with no shoes, no knickers and no handkerchiefs. For my brother and I things had not been as bad as this, although the only handkerchiefs we ever had were unhemmed pieces of rag. Also my sisters regarded "the vegetable man" as a person who was socially superior to us. He sold "King Edwards" which were a superior kind of potato. Assuming that Boyce's position had remained the same, then ours was considerably lower.

Very high in our social hierarchy was the rent collector. He was stout and rather short and trod heavily in the hall before coming down into our kitchen. Our rent was twenty-five shil

74

lings a week and I remember my mother, with tears running down her face, emptying the contents of her old leather purse on to the table. There simply wasn't enough. I could not believe that we should really be turned out. We were not. The rent man suddenly became human. He reduced our rent by half a crown. My mother's tears dried, but she looked old and drawn. Later my sister Pamela deliberately frightened my mother by imitating the rent man's heavy tread in the hall.

We were punished, usually, not in proportion to the crime we had committed but according to the amount of strain my mother was undergoing at the time. There had been no cane in Arundel Square and I do not remember it in Ellington Street, before the babies were born. We hated the cane. I used to poke the fire with it so that the end was all blackened. My sister Daphne hid it on top of the lavatory cistern, but when my mother said that the next person to need it must buy it with his own penny, and the next person was my brother, she found it again.

Daphne, the little one, frequently indulged in acts of mischief. It was she who locked the lavatory door on the outside and went to school with the key. Between her and me there was a special kind of affinity, partly through our close association in her infancy and partly through similarity of circumstance. She was the elder twin at birth and considerably the smaller, so that my mother felt that she had not done so well by the little one and consequently did not like her so much. I, as a baby, was very ill and nearly died. So strongly did my mother feel about this that she never mentioned it, but my father did. He said that as I was their first child, they had little idea of how to look after me and he thought I must have suffered. It was this that held Daphne and me together; that we were both something of a reproach to our mother and therefore not so well accepted by her. We have the same kind of toughness and lack of conventionality, although Daphne has a tender generosity of spirit which is lacking in me.

My sisters had much in common too, as "identical" twins are supposed to have. Somehow my mother contrived that they should be dressed alike and they were always together. Through this they received a good deal of attention and notice, but they nevertheless each regarded the other with some irritation. The business of their hair almost amounted to a major emotional crisis. When quite young they wore it long, as I had done. Then Daphne demanded that they should have it cut. Pamela wanted to keep hers long. But what they both wanted passionately, and what my mother wanted, was that they should continue to look alike. I do not remember the outcome then, but the incident is illustrative of their ambivalent attitude.

In character they were not "identical" at all but seemed more complementary. When they started school at Westbourne Road it was Pamela who was always running home, while Daphne was deputed to remain with her and see that she did not. This usually meant that they both absconded, for Daphne was very tenacious. Once I tried to take her to the dentist and would have succeeded, but it was Armistice Day and she used the two minutes' silence to attach herself to some railings as though she were the stronger half of a giant octopus. Some navvies noticed us, laughed and shouted: "Go it, young 'un!"

I enjoyed looking after the babies when people smiled at me and said how good I was and looked with approval from their windows as I pushed the pram up and down. When they gave moral support to my hoydenish young sister whom I could not control, I felt differently. By the time I got her to the dentist we were too late.

This sort of thing did not happen very often. The whole family adored the twins and never regarded them as anything but an asset. When they were about two years old an acquaintance of ours, a rich woman owner of several public houses, offered to adopt one of them. (Many people were genuinely anxious to help the unemployed in one way or another.) I shall never forget the utter incredulity of my brother and I when our parents told us about this. I said: "What! Give one away so that they wouldn't be twins any more?" And my brother exclaimed: "What! *Give* one away—for nothing?"

We could not imagine that anyone should expect us to be so stupid. Our parents knew this and told us about it merely in order to watch our incredulous amazement. We owned and consumed very little, but the best of all that came into that house went to the two youngest. My brother and I never questioned that this should be so. All that we felt we had missed ourselves, we wanted for "the children". Something of this feeling I had for my brother, although it had then been mixed with jealousy and rivalry. Certainly at five I had considered myself too old to have red for my favourite colour and always allowed my brother to have it. After the babies were born we quickly became "too old" for many of the things that children love.

For a time my mother took in work that she could do at home. She sewed the buttonholes on factory-made coats. And, in class, we read "The Song of the Shirt". I looked at my mother's eyes. They *were* red. I could not bear it and went to bed to cry. But I read "The Song of the Shirt" over and over again.

At school our form was divided into those who were "grown up" and those who were not. It was a matter of great interest and a constant topic of conversation. We exaggerated it all shamelessly and pretended to be in pain whether we were or not. Almost the only people who were practical and helpfully informative about it were the Jewesses. Stoke Newington was not far away and many Jewish people were in business there and sent their daughters to our school. I was but vaguely aware that their outlook was different from ours and better in its frank acceptance. Only much later did I come to realise how much I was affected by contact with these girls and the women of their families.

At home we had no bathroom. Baths were occasionally taken in a large zinc vessel that was set on pads of newspapers in front of the kitchen fire, but, as we grew older, this became more and more difficult, for the kitchen was our living-room too.

I was just prepared for a bath when I realised that I was menstruating. This had not happened to me before and I did not know what to do. At school there were many taboos concerning monthly periods; one must not go swimming, eat ice-cream, wash in cold water, do gym, nor have a bath. But I had never discussed it with my mother and the shock was too great for me to want to do so now. Besides, half the family had been sent out of the house and my mother was upstairs with the twins. Trembling, I had my bath as quickly as possible. I was almost certain that I should die. Everyone else in my form at school, next day, was almost certain too. I sat in my desk, doubled up,

77

with my hands across my stomach, as everybody else did at such times. My friends looked at me with sympathy. Several of them asked me if I felt all right. Unfortunately for the drama of the situation, I did.

About four weeks later I began to feel worried because it did not happen again. I knew all about it, of course, although I was not sure whether the months should be lunar or calendar. I thought that I had harmed myself for life and was sure that the final consequences would be terrible. I must be grown up; I had to bring it on somehow. I jumped down the basement stairs and then broke some of the springs of the prickly green sofa by turning somersaults on it. After this the room began to reel. It was, of course, the old equilibrium trouble, but I did not connect it and thought that the dizziness was a symptom of the dire disease I had caused in myself.

I did have another period but, by then, nobody at school found it so interesting because, most inappropriately, nothing awful had happened to me. Only Sonia was troubled because, she said, I must tell my mother and I could not see that this was necessary. The holidays began and still I had not told her. Sonia wrote me an urgent, anxious letter which I read and put away at the bottom of my sewing-box. My mother took out the letter and read it. She always did this, but I had not yet had enough letters of my own to realise that she did it. She told me that she had found my letter by accident, and asked what it was that Sonia wanted me to tell her. It took nearly a whole day to get it out of me. Then she said: "Is it that you've started or just that you know about it?" I said I had known about it since I was eight, and it struck me suddenly that she knew nothing at all of our school life, our conversations and our interests. She said that, during a period, I must not eat ice-cream, go swimming, wash in cold water, and have a bath, and any respect that I had had for her vanished as did my confidence in her. I resolved then that for my sisters it should be different.

One of the pastimes in which Sonia and I indulged and which must have caused some inconvenience to our friends and relatives was to call on them at almost any time. We had reached that stage in our relationship when we "told each other everything" and we regarded people whom we knew and who

78

mattered to us, at the time, rather as we regarded exhibits in a personal snapshot album which might be brought out occasionally for the benefit of an intimate friend. It was in this way that Sonia took me to show me the Waterton's.

They lived at Surbiton and Alice Waterton's brother had been a close friend of Sonia's mother. Donald Waterton was even then becoming well known as a child psychiatrist and we had both read his book on *Disorders of Childhood*. He was fair, with violet eyes and a light and pleasing voice. I liked him instantly.

Sonia was in love with "Aunt Alice". We called it "having a pash". She was a tall dignified woman, whom I remember as being dressed mostly in lovat green. She used to make pottery and paint pictures and the house contained a studio and a pottery-room. I had never seen such rooms in a house before, nor even heard of anything like them.

I never really saw that house at its best for, when we arrived, they were preparing to move to Pilgrim's Lane in Hampstead. I rather think that we called on them there too, before they had had time to remove the dust-sheets, and each piece of furniture bore a tiny label to show where it must be put.

Another social activity in which Sonia was able to indulge was that of asking to tea the various objects of our adolescent passion. Sonia's mother seemed always willing to entertain them and even to write them letters of invitation. I too was invited, for the whole proceeding gave rise to the kind of excitement which is doubled when it is shared.

I do not know by what means Sonia persuaded her mother to allow Sonia and me to go on holiday alone. Perhaps the idea seemed to be too attractively convenient for her to need much persuading, and I think that the only time our mothers ever met was over the arrangements for this. We were to go to a village in Norfolk, by coach, and I was to sleep at Hendon the night before.

I was given Sonia's bedroom and lay staring at the moon. Sonia's mother had a forceful personality and a peculiar insensitiveness to the feelings of others, particularly children. She would, perhaps, point out obliquely that I had my bread and butter in the wrong hand and should, in any case, have put it on my plate. I, being new to this kind of behaviour, would be consumed with embarrassment and she would wonder at my expression of misery. So great was my feeling of tension in her house that I did not sleep at all that night and, at two o'clock, sat on the window-sill and read Darwin's *Origin of Species* by moonlight. The moon crept away like a snail that leaves a rim of silver on a stone, and I saw the sky, all wan in grey gossamer, blush at its own awakening. Next day I had shingles, but we did not know what they were. We were on our own by then and did nothing about it.

All of that holiday we spent talking, as we went along country lanes; on to the beach at Cromer, and into Norwich. Sometimes, out of doors we sang songs in two parts. I think that a really happy childhood must be constantly as that holiday was for me, blissful and almost unremembered.

At Hendon, I really began to be conscious of music and became interested in the lives of some composers. In that house there were busts all over the place and a death-mask of Beethoven whom Sonia's mother seemed to me to resemble. We had a piano at home but I did not like it because it was never in tune. I did not quite understand this. What I knew was that certain notes played together, on the piano at Sonia's house, produced a kind of wave rhythm which I could recognise and which I liked. On the piano at home this did not happen.

For a time I had bought second-hand books with most of my pocket money and found that in English literature lessons at school I had at least a nodding acquaintance with almost any author that was mentioned. To me these books had seemed valuable beyond price. They must have seemed almost priceless to the bookseller too, for he rarely charged more than sixpence each. Now I bought music, struggled through Beethoven sonatas, analysed harmony. We had a new music mistress. She started a class in musicianship. This was an "extra" and my parents could not pay for me to join, but, with the connivance of this teacher, I went all the same.

During this time I actively disliked my brother, as he did me; we fought as the cats never did. When we were very young, I had been his superior in everything. By the time he was ten and a half and I was twelve I found I could only just beat him at running. After that I lost interest and would not race any more.

My brother had one physical weakness of which I always took advantage when we fought; his nose bled very easily. I do not think this hurt him much, but the feel and the sight of the blood always unnerved him and he would have to give in. This was one of the few aspects of my life which Sonia did not share. She had never been struck in her life, nor witnessed nor taken part in any kind of physical violence, a circumstance which was incomprehensible to me.

I hated my body. I had grown fat and felt that, apart from my hands, I was coarse and ugly. My mother, although she was fairly tall, looked like a barrel propped on two spindly legs. It is the kind of figure one often sees in middle-aged women amongst the very poor. My father was broad-shouldered but lean, spare as the leg of a crow. When a boy he had stolen the collar from a dog that was reputed to be fierce and he had worn that collar as a belt. At twelve he worked, cleaning out furnaces, he being thin enough to squeeze through the doors. His dinner was a farthingsworth of potatoes a day. My mother was quite definite in her ideas regarding our well-being; she considered that we were better fed the more we had to eat, well-grown if we were heavy, and sensibly clad if we wore as much as possible.

She worked according to two rules; that we should wear more clothes than anyone else we knew and that the twins should be dressed to look alike. The amount of resourcefulness and ingenuity that the latter required was formidable, but she managed it so well that sometimes even my father could not tell which was which. All her spare time she spent sewing and when, at the welfare centre, she won a prize for a "renovation" she chose to have a length of material with which to make dresses for her twins because, in all the four years of their lives, they had worn nothing new. She made even their hats which were trimmed with celluloid cherries like her own (except that, as we found, their cherries were hollow and hers were stuffed with a kind of cotton wool).

My father's views on these things were in almost complete opposition to my mother's. He never said anything, but his general attitude and his whole way of living proclaimed it. After the age of about six, and without thinking very much about it, my brother and I had accepted our father's standards, in this, rather than our mother's. There was never a battle but we exerted constant pressure on her to let us go without socks, without overcoats, without hats. It was of no use, for these first two things were a matter of principle with her, the last a matter of pride. She wore so many clothes herself that my brother once tried with a pin to find out how deep was the aggregate of layers. To us, fatness was almost indecent and our ideal was something like our father when he was young, something like D'Artagnan, something like Robin Hood, and something like a Red Indian, tall, spare, tough as cowhide and needing little of anything.

I suppose by some standards I was not really fat but I was plumper than I had ever been, and it filled me with disgust as well as giving my brother something to mock at. Besides, although the Sioux-D'Artgnan ideal was beginning to lose some of its romance for me, another ideal was forming and that was represented by the eighteenth-century poets, those who, like Shelley, had died young. I "lost" my tie so that the collar of my school blouse gaped Byronically. I was determined to die by the time I was thirty and to look pale and ethereal for most of the years preceding this. I learnt that Byron had fed himself on rice and vinegar in order to achieve such an effect and I tried to do the same. It was no use. My mother did not like it and several hours a week spent on the games field, avoiding the ball, gave me an appetite which I had not the will power to deny. I gave up the struggle, read Boswell's *Life of Johnson*, ate like a hog and refused to wash because it was warmer to remain dirty.

Sonia did not share my love of literature. Our identification one with another broke down over this. Sonia liked reading. She loved stories and characters. She liked people. But I loved words. At this time I found poetry most interesting and spent hours studying prosody and experimenting with verse forms of my own. I had a pash on the English mistress. She was a dumpy little thing between forty and fifty. She wore blue and her hair was that pale gold that fades imperceptibly to silver. For a time all my essays were in verse, addressed to a remote and unnamed lady. Then we were told that, unless instructed otherwise, our essays must be in prose. I found this so easy, after my struggles with rhyme and metre, that I covered pages with my small, close writing. The mistress then limited our essays to two hundred words. I became interested in sentence construction, for its own sake, and made it a point of honour that each of these two-hundred-word essays should contain no more than a single sentence, which I rippled with alliterations, made sonorous with onomatopœia and packed with imagery, that was the fruit of constant day-dreaming, until I had made a parody of a parody, a clumsy complexity of clause and phrase as involved as my limited ability allowed, and graced with at least one breathlessly exciting reference to "Dear Reader", in the innocent belief that my essay would be seen by no one but the English mistress and that, even then, my device might prove too subtle for her understanding, so that it was necessary, sometimes, to add, also, a poem written to an unknown, unnamed goddess, a mysterious and omnipotent "she". I always got high marks for my English essays.

In spite of all this I began to enjoy the simplicity of some of the Russian writers. I had discovered Tolstoy, at Hendon, and read *War and Peace* over a period of about two years, but I enjoyed equally Tolstoy's folk tales which I read to my sisters. Both Turgenev and Tchekov I regarded as more sophisticated than the English authors we studied at school. At the same time I became acquainted, too, with Lewis Carroll, A. A. Milne and a number of other writers for children that I had not known in my own childhood, but which I found now in the public library and read to my sisters. I remember making lists and grading these books carefully according to the way in which I felt the understanding of the children would develop. Occasionally they would ask me what I was reading myself and I would try to translate the themes of these Russian writers into language that a four-year-old could understand. After one attempt of mine to explain Dostoevsky my sister Pamela said she would like to change her name to "Idiot".

# CHAPTER VI

## IN PURSUIT OF OUR IDEALS

O U R main preoccupation at school was with our romantic
attachments to members of the teaching staff and, occasionally, to prefects, although the latter occurred less as we got older.
The chief aim in these "affairs" was to meet the object of one's
passion out of school. Sonia was more successful in this than
anyone because she was in a position to issue invitations, which
most of us were not. But I did have a certain amount of success
myself because I was so much more obviously deprived, and a
number of people were moved by the desire to "take me in hand"
or to offer me such adjuncts to culture as art exhibitions, concerts, music clubs and, more rarely, a cinema show or a visit to
a theatre. (I was stage-struck, of course, although I liked only
Shakespeare.) We were not satisfied by these more conventional
activities and tried to supplement them by some of our own.
We found extraordinary ways of making our way homewards.
It was often rather like going from London to Bristol by way of
Glasgow.

Two of the mistresses in whom we were interested used to go
part of the way home on one of the number nineteen buses. This
route terminated at Highbury Barn and there the buses used to
wait. A row of bus conductors and drivers stood leaning against
the wall. We calculated that if we waited with them and got on
to a bus only when our mistresses came into view, it would be
too obvious to them that we had waited purposely. The only
way was to sit on the bus so that it would look as though we had
intended to go by it anyhow.

We sat for about five minutes. The conductor stepped on. But
our mistresses had not arrived. This was of no use at all, so we
jumped off. When the first bus had gone we sat in the next one.
We sat in a whole succession of buses. At last a conductor who

had apparently been watching us told us that we could pay for sitting in them. He pushed us back. The bus went on and we went with it. As we bowled slowly down Highbury Grove we saw our teachers, who had apparently decided to walk through the "Fields". We hung about round Highbury Corner for a while, but it soon became obvious that we had missed them, so we went home.

This was only one of many similar escapades, some of which entailed waiting for two or three hours outside the houses of our loved ones. One teacher, in particular, showed a good deal of interest in me. She talked to me for hours and asked me why I would not work. She said I would have been as good as anyone in the form if only I would do as I was told. I gloried in the attention I was getting and did not even bother to think why I did practically nothing all the term. Sometimes I became interested in the work for its own sake, not for marks. This happened most often when we had been set a piece of homework that nobody could do. Other girls would ask me about it and then I would try to do it, working at it, sometimes, for an hour or two. Usually I managed it, and passed it round, but I never bothered to give mine in.

The fact was that I did not care much about being as good as anyone in the form. What I did want was to be in the sixth form, working for "Intermediate" and then to go on to university, but I knew this was impossible for me. I was lucky to have remained at school even as long as I had. Towards the end of our third year at Highbury, both Titch and Violet seemed to have "faded out". They did not "leave school" with a kind of triumphal launching as most did. They simply ceased to be there any longer, and nobody knew anything about them. They were never my special friends at the High School, but I thought about them sometimes, though I never saw them after they left.

I went once, with my current passion, to a cinema one Saturday. The film was at the "Dominion" in Tottenham Court Road, but I went first to her flat for lunch. Part of her kitchen was very narrow and I held her as I pushed by. She brushed me away, turned to face me and said, in a tense way, that I must not do that. I asked why not and she said: "Because it might develop into an unhealthy relationship." It was two years before I discovered what an "unhealthy relationship" was. In the bus I took her hand, but, having taken it, I did not know what to do with it. I sat, playing with her fingers until she pointed out that she had five of them on that hand. In the cinema I tried again, but she remarked that she had five fingers on that hand too, and I began to giggle. For the rest of the time I sat shaking while she looked at me. I do not remember anything about the film.

I had left her and turned to go along Oxford Street, when I saw ahead of me the somewhat formidable figure of the head-mistress, who was a Miss Kyle. She spoke to me formally, about the weather, I believe. I went on, but could not avoid giving a backward look towards the mistress I had just left, and saw her breathlessly making her way towards "Kylo". I heard her say: "Did you want to speak to me, Miss Kyle?" and Kylo answering that she didn't think so, with a look of polite surprise.

Kylo was an enormous, dignified, matriarchal figure. She always wore black and, although she was nearing retirement age, had a rich coil of hair that shone like jet. One morning of the following week she gave us a talk during notices, after prayers. She said she did not like the way in which some of us walked along the street. People who behaved properly did not touch each other in public. We did not see her, Miss Kyle, walk-ing along with her arm round Miss Jaggs's neck. A murmur of excitement ran through the school and Jaggy, who, at fifty-odd, was rather attractive, smiled and looked down. Kylo said that if one were escorting a person who was old or infirm one might assist them by taking their arm and one might lead a small child by the hand, but there was no need for any other kind of contact.

One of the girls at school organised a group for drama and elocution. Her name was Alice Greenberg and her father was a tailor in Stoke Newington. My accent had improved a good deal at Highbury and I overheard the parents of some of my friends say that I "spoke quite well, considering everything". But Alice thought differently. She was dark and extremely pretty, two or three years older than I, self-assured, competent and, in the matter of diction, uncompromising. We spent many half-hours together in opposite corners of an empty classroom while she, metaphorically, tore me to pieces, and then carefully built up my confidence again.

We had decided to put on a performance of *Quality Street*, but when we announced this, after much of the work had already been done on it, we were told that it was "unsuitable". No other explanation was given and, at the next meeting of the drama society, we came to the conclusion that *Quality Street* reflected too accurately the condition of the mistresses themselves for them to want us to give a performance of it. Instead we put on *The Poetasters of Isphahan* which seemed to be acceptable to everyone.

So far the friendship between Sonia and me had not been regarded kindly by anyone in authority over us; her mother objected for obvious reasons, and mine objected because it was felt that from Sonia I was "getting big ideas". At school the relationship was frowned upon, for Sonia's sake, and the blame for those of our escapades that were found out was laid at my door. We were put in different forms. This meant that whereas, previously, we had been able to spend "study" periods together in conversation, now they rarely coincided. It was unthinkable that either of us should spend such a period not in the company of the other, so we began to "skip" lessons. This was fairly easy to do; we had got used to doing it for gym, to which neither of us ever went, after our first year. The remark on our school reports for this subject was always the same: "Fair". In the other subjects, it was a simple matter to get an outline of the lesson from another girl and I never did any homework anyway. The penalty for this was the loss of a conduct mark and I grew to regard this as a system of exchange and automatically deducted a conduct mark from myself for every exercise I did not do. When it was discovered that I had been doing this without any reference to any member of staff, people became annoyed.

Loss of conduct marks counted "against the house". I was not interested in "the house" except during the time that the captain was a prefect on whom I had a "pash" and thus I received more attention from her the more badly I behaved. A system of after-school detentions was started, but I did not go. "Fatigue" drill was instituted in which we were exercised until our muscles ached. I went only once to see what it was like. Soon parents objected and it was stopped.

About this time Sonia went to live with Donald Waterton and his wife at Hampstead. We were greatly excited by this, because of Sonia's romantic attachment for Alice Waterton, and the Hampstead house was a wonderful place to which to ask people to tea.

The Watertons had two maids, one of whom was called Annie, because her name, too, was Alice, which would have been confusing. I felt vaguely resentful about this. We used to sit in the kitchen sometimes to talk to Annie and Gwen and to listen to their wireless. It was only after several weeks that one of the disadvantages of having domestic servants began to dawn on me.

I had been invited to Hampstead, and we stood on the door-step making last-minute arrangements in whispers. We nearly always did this, wherever we went, partly because we were usually engaged in some sort of intrigue and partly for me to receive final instructions as to how I should behave. The latter was very important, at this juncture, because "Aunt Alice" had obviously had some misgivings about accepting me as a friend for Sonia. The arithmetic helped. Besides, my accent was, by now, quite passable. While we were standing there, whispering, the door was suddenly flung open, and there was Annie all angry and starched in her afternoon uniform. She asked us what we were doing, standing on the doorstep like that. Why hadn't we rung the bell? We said we were just going to, and she answered that we were being a very long time about it.

During the evening Aunt Alice taught us to dance. She waltzed with each of us in turn, while she hummed. Then she told us to dance together and she would play the piano. To begin with we enjoyed it, but she went on and on. I think she forgot about us. We did not know what to do. In the end we sat down, just out of her range of vision and shuffled our feet in time to the music. This was almost as tiring, after a while, as dancing.

Later that evening, just before dinner, I found myself sitting alone in the dining-room. I cannot imagine why this should have been so nor what Sonia can have been doing that I should not have been with her, but as I sat waiting the lift came up from the kitchen. The lift was full of silver. I thought that, at any moment, one of the maids would come in and begin to lay the table. Minutes passed and no one came. It occurred to me that Annie knew that I was in the dining-room and would empty the lift for her, but I was always in doubt about this sort of thing. So often had I given way to impulse and helpfully performed some chore that should have been left to the maids. Mostly, it seemed to me, that it was easier, quicker and pleasanter to do it oneself than to "ring", but I was, by now, acutely sensitive and hated making social *faux pas*. I began to prickle all over with the sensation that I called "nausea of the flesh". I sat there in misery, unable to move, rooted in indecision, like cement. Nobody came. And suddenly the tension broke. I jumped up, on the impulse, and took two heavy strides towards the lift. It descended, as I reached it, and I remembered too late that the signal for its return was two firm stamps on the dining-room floor. The thumping tread of an overweight adolescent must have sounded just like that.

The Watertons had suggested to Sonia that she should go to a different school, a girls' public school. This proposal dismayed us. Sonia was adamant about it and refused their offer. Whatever the advantages, to either of us, or both, we did not want to be parted.

Neither of us had any illusions about the other, nor yet about ourselves, for we quarrelled occasionally. All of Sonia's tremendous energy was poured into her own particular kind of exhibitionism. She was wholly egotistical and so jealous that I used to conceal from her most of my achievements until I knew she had something which she could score off against them. One often hears of success changing its victims, of their becoming too proud to continue to see old friends. Knowing Sonia, I could not help feeling that some of the fault might be in the friends themselves. When I first broadcast, it was almost more than she could bear.

I had an enormously inflated idea of my own powers and sensibilities. I was insufferably conceited, intolerably self-opinionated and far too frequently right. I was excruciatingly shy and spent most of my time, in company, in dumb embarrassment, which seemed churlish and ill-mannered. I was also hopelessly inept about travelling, telephoning or getting anywhere on time.

Almost the only quality we had in common was a lack of inhibition, while we were together. Each of us was that extreme kind of personality, so introverted as to seem extrovert, the kind that is communicative to an almost indecent degree, because it is so little troubled by the reactions of other people. It is rather the attitude that Cleopatra had towards her slaves when she went through all the intimate routine of her toilet in their presence, because she was totally unaware of them, as human beings. It is an attitude that becomes modified as one leaves adolescence. When Sonia died it was almost impossible to talk of it to anyone who had not known us both. There was nothing "good" that I could say about her. Our friendship was not based on mutual admiration and I rather doubt if real friendships ever are. There was just something in each of us that responded to the other. We were two badly deprived children who found comfort in being nearly always together. A fortnight before she died and when she knew I was writing this book, we spent some weeks together. Sonia talked incessantly of our early days, giving me all the reminiscences that I needed, as though this were just one of the things it was necessary for her to put in order. And all the memories came back to her, all her past life, and ours, as though, already, she was drowning. It was one of the most heart-breaking things that she should do this for me, and I would have given worlds to have had her back again with all her jealousy, with all her fierce vitality. This way it was as though she were already dead.

Sometimes, at school, we had "students" to teach us, young post-graduates whose main effect was to start a new outbreak of "pashes". It was unfortunate for me that one of these should have come to take English and that, when I gave in my usual essay, daringly sprinkled with "dear reader's", I did not know that it would be marked by her, but it was—with two thin red lines across the page. I had been here before. I remembered the verb "to be" and the ideas I had built up around it. Now it had become a verb like any other.

I went up to her, in front of the form, and asked her why she had marked my essay like that. I knew what she would say and, because of this, the incident was imbued with a kind of artificiality that was wholly comic. If ever a student teacher responded unsuitably to being "played up" that one did. I began to giggle. So did the rest of the form. There was a trace of panic behind the student's rimless spectacles. She asked me where I had got my essay.

"I wrote it."

"Not out of your own head."

"Yes, I did."

"I thought you had taken it from one of the Essays of Elia." The rest of the form laughed more loudly. They knew about the "Dear Reader".

"Which of the Essays of Elia?"

"I thought, perhaps, 'Dream Children'."

"But, if I had, you would have been able to find it, wouldn't you?"

The room was suddenly quiet. It looked as though I was going to "go too far". I often did, but nothing came of it. The student said: "I'm afraid I didn't try to find it. I assumed at once that you hadn't written it yourself."

I answered casually that I always wrote like that, and she asked me if I had been reading much of Charles Lamb lately. I said I had been reading De Quincey. Then the student teacher told me that if I liked to copy out my essay again, she would give me a mark for it. I might have been annoyed about this; it meant extra work and I did not like work, and also the mistake had not been mine, but I was too much amused, too pleased at the opportunity to show off. I could not give an essay mark to my form mistress and told her, grinning, that there had been a misunderstanding and I would get my mark as soon as possible. It was weeks before I eventually rewrote that essay, and I did it then only because I was told that I should lose the marks altogether if I did not. Full marks for an essay meant a "distinction" which I coveted, in this subject only, but in the end I found I had lost two marks for spelling.

Another of the students who came to Highbury was Stella Jackson. She taught French and we found her fascinating. Nearly everybody did. She wore sandals, full skirts and bright shirt blouses, buttoned very low. Out of doors she wore a voluminous black cloak. Her hair was cut in the style of a boy of the sixteenth century and was the colour of birch leaves in autumn. She looked like a birch tree, slim and beautifully shaped with fine wrists and ankles and her clothes seemed somehow to cling to her, so that one saw her naked. Sonia asked her to tea, and we spent many hours riding "home" on the tops of buses with her. We rode nearly all over central London; for her, life was exciting and she seemed never to be going to the same place two evenings running.

Stella Jackson seemed not to mind our presence. Sometimes she took us out in the evenings and, in a vegetarian restaurant, she introduced us to Michael Campbell. He was a man of about thirty, with regular features, fine dark eyes, and smooth, white hair above a young face. All his movements were extraordinarily graceful. He had a wonderfully resonant middle-register voice and liquid diction. Stella and Michael seemed to be together quite a lot. They were interested in psychology and economics as well as in food values.

To our dismay Stella remained at Highbury for only one term and then caught scarlet fever. She did not return to the school, but she kept in touch with Sonia and we both saw her and Michael quite often.

Our study periods at school were becoming a problem. People had begun to notice that we were sometimes to be found in places not listed on our time-table. Our absence from class was not noticeable, but our presence at the wrong time in such places as the library, the wash-rooms or the art-room was. We were not allowed to go into the lavatories together, it being carefully explained that some of us might be undergoing "certain physical changes" that it was inadvisable for the younger ones to know about. The explanation was invalid for several reasons, but the rule was strictly enforced all the same. The difficulty was, therefore, to find a place for our "study" where no one would think of looking for us.

Our favourite place, and one which for several terms was not discovered, was the specimen cupboard attached to the biology laboratory. A large window gave on to the centre courtyard, and the "cupboard" was warm and light. An array of green plants graced the window-sill and the shelves opposite and, at one time, a glass tank containing goldfish stood on the floor. We used to crouch beside this tank, for there was nothing to sit on, and if we stood up we could be seen above the foliage by anybody looking out of one of the corridor windows opposite.

One morning we had been there for one lesson period when the bell rang for break. We were comfortable where we were and saw no reason why we should go down into the playground, so we remained. The bell went for the end of break. There was a pounding on the stairs and a swinging of doors. The biology laboratory was often used as a passage-way from one side of the building to the other. There was an ominous scraping of stools. I looked through the keyhole. People were sitting on the stools. They were not using the laboratory as a passage-way; they had come for a lesson. The biology mistress came into the room. After this we could not talk in anything louder than the faintest whisper. We took it in turns to look through the keyhole, although Sonia's "turns" were longer than mine, for the biology mistress was her current "pash". The lesson was on "osmosis", the only botany lesson I really remember. There was an experiment with an egg membrane. One extracted all the meat from the egg, carefully and delicately and through a single small hole. Then one dissolved the shell in vinegar so that nothing was left but a little bag of skin, empty and with a hole in it and soon to become stiff, crumpled and discoloured if left for long out of water.

The end of the period came. The bell went. Our nerves screwed to an excruciating pitch because, in a moment, the tension would be released. The class in the laboratory would go, the mistress would walk out, and we could dash off to sit in our respective form rooms innocently as though nothing had happened, as though we had not spent the last two periods hiding in the specimen cupboard.

Nobody moved. The voice of the mistress went on. It was a double period.

In our agitation we had stood up. Now we saw, across the courtyard, a group of girls who had noticed us and understood our predicament. They could see through the windows of the biology laboratory, the room full of girls, the mistress; they could see us, standing there guiltily with only a thin partition between us and discovery. Sonia's pash on the biology mistress was well known. All the implications and ramifications of our situations were evident in their excited faces. We began to feel apprehensive. They would not inform about us; nobody ever did; but it did seem as though they might betray us by their manner and their gesticulations. Suddenly they rushed off and we knew that, soon, the story would be all over the school.

We crouched down again. The lesson went on. Little bags of membrane that become distended as they fill with liquid, was not the most comfortable subject for our thoughts, at that moment. By the end of this period we should have been in the cupboard for two and a half hours. Our need was becoming desperate. There was a sink in the specimen cupboard, but it was high up, right in front of the window. Even though everyone else was probably now in class, to use the sink was more than we dared. Apart from this there was only the tank for the goldfish. Soon the lesson would be over, when the bell went again, then the class would disperse and we should be free. This episode would become just another of the things that we had managed to get away with. I looked through the keyhole again. This stage in the experiment was over. Now on the end of a glass tube, the egg membrane, half filled with strong sugar solution, was suspended in water.

It happened in a matter of seconds; the mistress stepped off her platform and strode towards our door. We leapt up and stood facing it. She was so surprised when she saw us that we half expected her to drop the apparatus, but almost at once she resumed the schoolmistress pose and said in a voice that rang like a glass bell jar:

"What are you doing in here?"

We said we were studying.

"There are other places provided for your study. Go!"

The class gave such a gasp as we emerged it would have sucked in the walls, if the windows had been closed, and we went at such a rate that we were down the third flight of stairs before the swing door slammed for the first time.

Our apprehension during the next few days was hideous. We were not sent for, either by the biology mistress or the head.

No letter was sent home to our parents. We were not expelled. In fact, apart from the announcement, during a lesson, that the goldfish had died, nothing more happened at all.

We lived almost perpetually in this state of high excitement which only a few of the other girls shared to a limited degree. It was as though we saw, all the time, a different world, vivid, teeming, unpredictable; glowing with the brilliant and exotic vegetation of our own feelings, warmed by our eagerness, and lit with our delight. It was a kind of tropical, submarine existence or a world of equatorial caves.

During the time that Sonia lived with the Watertons she and I did not go on holiday alone, but we did all go together, Dr. and Mrs. Waterton, Sonia and I. They came to fetch me in Donald's Rolls-Royce tourer and, while I got ready, Donald stood on the doorstep of our house in order to watch his car. Sonia and I sat in the open back of the car wrapped in rugs. We stayed in a very small boarding-house in Norfolk and only these incidents remain in mind. One is of Alice showing us a bird. It was a yellowhammer, perched on the tipmost branch of a shrub. I remember Alice laying her hair against mine and saying: "Look! Can you see his little yellow head?"

Until then I had not really believed that there were any birds but sparrows, pigeons, and what I thought of as black-birds, but which were probably starlings. A new field of interest was suddenly opened to me, as it had been with the little frogs, a new source of wonder and now a nostalgic longing. It was because of this feeling, in spite of all I read and enjoyed reading, that I could not look at travel books. The depression caused by them was too great. Only when I was much older, had walked over all of England, and begged my passage to Europe on small cargo boats, could I find stimulus in this longing and not a smarting frustration.

Another memory was of going, with Sonia, into a green field in the freshness of early morning and seeing Donald, slim and fair, brown-skinned and dressed in white, and standing in the sunshine under the dappling trees. We ran towards him and he opened his arms and ran towards us.

Sonia and I shared a bedroom in that country house. It was the one designed to accommodate the daughters of the family and Donald and Alice had the "parent" room, through which we had to pass to reach ours.

I was absorbed at this time by a new physical sensation. I had known it before, but not with climactic intensity. I connected this with poetic ecstasy. I thought about it mostly at night so that when I was lying in bed in that little country house it was the first time I had been conscious of it in the presence of another person. It was one of those things, like the writing, that I had not been able to share with Sonia, but there seemed no reason why I should not do so. I began to describe it to her. She sat up in bed, considerably alarmed. She asked if I was feverish, was I shivering, had I a temperature? I said it was not like that at all. It was a nervous thing, an agony, poetry, and exquisite joy.

"But you said it was physical!"

"Yes, it is, but—it isn't, not wholly . . ."

It was of no use. Sonia did not understand and I was more than ever convinced of the close association between this feeling and poetry, my love for which I knew she did not share. I did not connect the feelings with Sonia's rope.

Years later we discussed it, and I told her of this incident. She did not remember it, but she did recall a time when she had tried, in the same way, to convey those things to me and I had not been able to understand. With each other we seemed to have no inhibitions. There was nothing that we could not discuss. Yet, in this, at this time, however much we tried, in turn, there was simply no communication.

There were some relatives of Sonia's in Norfolk whom the Watertons decided to take us to visit. They lived in a vicarage not very far away from where we were staying. Everything about this vicarage seemed to be saying: "Once, long ago. . . ." Moss grew over the paths, like velvet covering the dead, and the hidden flower-beds swelled like tumuli, under the long grass. Excluding undergrowth knit together the dark shrubs in perpetual hibernation and out of the billows of knee-high grass which with the accumulation of years had dried out and bleached white, there thrust a brown wallflower, woody and branching and old. It was like looking down on to low cumulus. The house was of grey stone, half covered with old ivy and a cold veridian stain that had come creeping with the years. Two people lived in it, a father and son. The father was very old and the son quite young, only a little older than we were. They shared their name, which was Frederic, the father being "Fred" and the son "Eric". His mother was dead. She had borne many children (at the rate of about one a year, so rumour had it). They all died or were stillborn, except the last, whose birth she did not survive.

Fred was a bulky old man, with white hair, a clerical collar and great black gaps in his teeth. He took us in to show us the house, for no good reason that I can imagine. Immediately inside the heavy front door was a hall containing piles of books, a sea of papers and several oblong loaves of bread. There were books and one or two loaves on the staircase too, for the sides of the stairs seemed to be used like shelves. There was a meandering pathway between the things that were on them. Surreptitiously I trod on one of the loaves but without doing any apparent damage to it.

In the downstairs rooms, books were stacked against the walls. In none of these rooms was there anything on the floors but the papers; not in any of them.

Fred seemed to feel it incumbent upon him to show us everything and we herringboned our way up the stairs between the bread bricks and the books and the papers. It all looked like the archives section of a government department through which a tornado had passed and had been long stilled. Then Fred opened the door of the "nursery" and the atmosphere changed. It was as though, for eighteen years, this room had held its breath. The carpet lay under a quarter of an inch of dust. Soot reposed, like a fall of scree, near the chimney, and all the furniture rested under a bloom of dust, grey plush and the grey chiffon-silk of cobweb. There was the cot, just one, and there was the pram. None of it, so Fred told us, had been touched since his wife died. Perhaps we were his first visitors in that time, and that is why he showed it to us. Certainly he could hardly have shown it to anyone else, for the dry, soft desert of that room had been unmarked until we trod in it. In the cupboard there were clothes and, on the back of the door, a hat, where she had left it.

Fred seemed elated and this shocked me somewhat. I felt that a memory that had been revered for eighteen years should not then be met by anything louder than an awed silence. Perhaps he had been waiting, all this time, for just such a handful of people to come and see how faithful he was to his wife's memory. He told many jokes, and in each of them the point was lost in a burst of laughter, like the cracking of boulder-strewn earth in a field of burnt corn stubble. Tea, mercifully, was in the garden. Fred, in a thunder-split of laughter, shouted for "Mary Ann" and Eric came out, competently bearing a very large tray. The meal was surprisingly good. Even the bread was all right.

I thought of Eric and pitied him for many years.

This was my second experience of cultured Bohemianism. Until that year I had found that intellectual and æsthetic interests were always the concomitant of some degree of social graciousness. The two things had seemed to me inseparable. But Stella had begun to introduce us to the aggressive, left-wing political intellectuals, some of whom slept on the floor and ate vegetarian meals off orange-boxes. And in the large house with the two Frederics I saw the total rejection of at least half of all I had hoped to aspire to.

# CHAPTER VII

# MUSICIANSHIP AND THE BLUE CAFÉ

WHEN I was fourteen we moved to Fore Street, Edmonton, N.18. I do not remember the number of the house because it was a café and people always used the name of it in our address. The move came about in this way.

During the years when we lived in Ellington Street my father had had several periods of unemployment, the longest being three years, and a number of different jobs. The worst of these we were not told about and the conditions in the organised labour camps, when he lived away from us, I did not learn of until many years later. He also did crowd work in one or two films from which he came home to give us an exhibition of himself in tights and Flora Robson (whom he admired enormously) as Queen Elizabeth, trying to mount a horse side-saddle with the wrong foot in the stirrup. One Christmas he played the part of a monkey in a pantomime. But tights did not suit him, the monkey skin was too small, and this kind of work, though satisfying in some respects, could not be relied on to support six people.

Our "superiority" was observed by many of our acquaintances in the intricate social hierarchy in which we lived. We were poor but we were very deserving, and the publican who wanted to appropriate my sister was not the only person to be moved by a desire to lift us out of our stony rut. A nursing sister, employed in one of the council services, decided, on retirement, to enter business. She bought the café and installed my parents to run it. My father did the work in the café while my mother cooked and let the rooms on the top floor. It seemed ideal.

In those days, if a family moved from one county to another, then a scholarship was automatically forfeited, so there was now trouble about my education. My father went up to the council house and made a fuss. I do not know how he did it, but I did not lose my scholarship, but continued at Highbury Hill High School, although Edmonton was officially in Middlesex, and I needed to travel backwards and forwards every day. I took a tram as far as the end of Blackstock Road and walked the rest. We were issued at school with special low-priced tickets for travelling. The fares were an added burden all the same.

At school, Sonia and I were engaged always in some kind of intrigue. This frequently involved long and immensely complicated stories, which we relayed to the current objects of our devotion. Sometimes these stories were excuses for our frequent defalcations; mostly they were merely attempts to dramatise ourselves. People accepted our flights of fancy with amusement. Nobody took us seriously and our inventions became more and more like the inflated nonsense published in the cheap and sensational girls' papers which, at that time, we never read. It was Sonia who miscalculated the good sense and general perspicacity of the teaching staff, and it still seems incredible to me that two teachers and the headmistress should have seized on one of these stories with the avidity of my Wanstead relatives reading the *News of the World* on a Sunday afternoon.

They did not question us, but wrote immediately to our parents. We admitted that there was no truth in the story and that we had made it up between us because we thought it exciting. The story reflected badly on me, but I do not think either of us thought about that. We never expected to be believed, anyway. But they talked of police and law courts and slander. My parents said that Sonia was "being shown up in her true colours", and the adults on her side contrived to make me feel that I was to blame for the whole thing. Nothing of all this seemed nearly so important as our being together. This was now forbidden. Sonia was made to write me a letter of apology, and when I saw it I wanted nothing so much as to laugh at it, with her, on the stairs of Hampstead Underground station.

It became obvious that, for the first time, the powers that be were going to enforce their ruling. We were now constantly watched. In the playground, we lingered about twenty feet apart. I brooded and lowered at the duty mistress. Sonia bit her finger-nails down to the quicks and then bit the quicks.

After some weeks of this, I gave up and sat in the library, reading, except when I was discovered and turned out "into the sunshine" which I loathed. It was summer and nobody understood why I did not want to be "out in this lovely weather", while I could not understand how anyone could think it pleasant to walk in the sunshine wearing pleated serge and black woollen stockings.

With Sonia, life had been twice as large and fifty times as bright. Alice Waterton had made the countryside live for me. Amongst dull hedges, ragged grass and drab, fidgety little birds, she found blackthorn and guelder rose, hazel and briar; darnel, meadow fescue and soft brome; screaming starlings, fighting jays, pert chaffinch and a skylark doing an Indian rope trick on a song. With Sonia it was people. Her intuition was remarkable, her observation was acute and there was always an undercurrent of communication and a greater intensity of meaning. This heightened significance was projected on to everything around, houses, streets, whole districts of London and still, to me, the smell and the sound of the London Underground gives a feeling of increased vitality and a sense that life is potentially rich and wonderful. To most of us, those older than ourselves were remote beings whose emotions, if they had any, were beyond our understanding. To Sonia (and occasionally to me) they were people whose own feelings were so strong that they could not sanction a performance of *Quality Street* by the children whom they taught.

The attitude of many towards their superiors is the attitude of Violet Leicester towards the bishop. Sonia's attitude was never this; she loved people because she found them human.

Now all that was over and life, for a while, was desolate and endless, like a beach that had been full of precious, uncut stones and now was full of pebbles.

There were distractions. I was given a free run of the art-room by our extraordinarily far-sighted art mistress, Nan Youngman, and, whereas before I had spent my free afternoons in conversation with Sonia, now I painted on great pieces of cardboard, in powder colours which I pounded together with gum. And there was music.

I used to go often to concerts and lectures for children at

Westminster. I had never gone with Sonia. She had a better sense of pitch than I but, because of her mother's profession, she did not really like music. It was my misfortune to have a very expressive face so that lecturers making, often, frustrated attempts to start discussion would remember having noticed me while they talked and would now point at me and suggest encouragingly: "You, I know, have something to say, haven't you?"

I had plenty to say, nearly always, but never the slightest wish to say it, and my voice, so carefully cultivated by Alice Greenberg, would vanish on these occasions, so that, in the end, I would have to go on to the platform, painfully self-conscious in my inked-over stockings, my outgrown tunic and my eccentric school hat, and whisper my comments into the lecturer's ear. Then he would repeat them out into the hall and to me they would sound completely daft.

This meant that I was often conspicuous at these talks and concerts. Everyone was extremely kind. Once or twice soloists remarked to me how pleasant it was to perform before faces that did not look completely wooden. I tried so hard to look just like that, but always got carried away by the music, with happy recognition at hearing a speaker express an idea I had already made my own, or with intolerant annoyance at something I did not agree with. Older and more confident young people would sometimes speak to me in the entrance hall and soon there were two people for whom I began to watch every week.

The girl Nicola was the younger of the two and a year or so older than I. She was lovely to look at and beautifully dressed. Having once noticed her, I could not look anywhere else, until the music began. Her brother was about two years older than she. He was very tall, nondescript, pasty-looking and with a nose that seemed to have melted and spread. He said their name was Mond and that he was Otis. It was as Nicola's friend that I began to visit their home, but I always felt that it was at her brother's instigation. I cannot imagine why, since I must have been extraordinarily unattractive. Perhaps he used to grow tired of looking at his lovely sisters. When they first invited me I said I did not know them, but Otis said that since we all attended the same musicianship class, we all knew each other. Soon I went quite often.

Nicola had the kind of personality that inspires and feeds on worship and I lived in a state of unremitting adoration.

"Of course, in this house you never know whether you are going to meet a dustman or a bishop." Mrs. Mond's voice sometimes sounded a little shrill. Even I knew that what she was saying was not quite true; if it had been she would not have mentioned it. I sensed that she was slightly unsure of herself. She was certainly unsure of me.

We on the lawn were engaged in one of those naïve and excessively intimate conversations beloved of adolescents. I said: "But how am I different?"

Nicola considered, then answered in her careless little voice: "You need education that's all."

"I won't be able to go on after matric."

Nicola regarded me with unmitigated scorn. "I don't mean that. I mean about things like changing in the afternoon and having a bath every night."

I answered: "If it's just being clean, you don't look very educated now," and Nicola mirthfully rolled on her back with her beautiful legs in the air. When she got up I added with some defiance: "I'm not dirty."

"No, but you have a funny smell. Your hair smells like the school kitchens."

"That's living in a café." Then I said bluntly: "Could you educate me?"

"No, but my mother could. Mary washes her hair late every night—terribly late."

We lay and watched Mary, Nicola's eighteen-year-old sister, walk across the loggia. Mary had passed that intangible barrier into the adult world and we talked of her in whispers.

That night, suddenly awake, I lay staring into the darkness which was full of pale gleam and black shadows. It teemed with little wriggling shapes like print that jostled on a page, like microscopic worms stirring in a culture. I liked the idea of the darkness as something fertile.

My bedroom was at the back of the house and only partly over the shop, nevertheless, I could hear the café filling up, the chairs scraping, the crockery rattling and the voices growing louder. I knew that tonight I should have to comfort the babies if the noise woke them.

I got out of bed and peered at the clock. It was half-past ten; the pubs would be closing. I climbed quietly back on to the bed and sat with my legs under the bedclothes, waiting.

The café had meant a great deal to us. It had altered our lives for a time. Now there was always meat for dinner and, in this way, every day was like a Sunday. We ate what was left after the café had been served and this was better than anything we had ever known. There was work now, solid, beneficient, remunerative work. In fact, there was far too much of it, but my parents had been starved of this kind of work for so many of the years of peace and depression that we welcomed it now as dry sand welcomes the rain.

The café was beautiful, pale blue and cream like sunshine in a summer sky. We stacked chairs, swept floors, wiped tables. We cooked until we all but melted in the heat, washed dishes until our fingers shrivelled and we served in the shop with our eyes bright and our feet quick with the wonder of it all.

I left my bed again and hung out of the window. The light shone out from the back of the shop with tinsel brilliance and stretched across the garden. The shop was growing noisier. People laughed loudly. I saw a man come out of the back way, slamming the door. He walked past the outside lavatory and, after a moment, began to urinate in the garden. I went in quickly. I was furious. Some part of me wanted to shout at him but I kept silent. When I heard him going back, I looked out again.

I crept through the darkness of the room, out of the door and half-way down the stairs to where I could see into the shop.

The café was transformed. Greasy fumes from the kitchen mingled with tobacco smoke. The air was like a poultice. I stared with stinging eyes through the grey scrim at my brother, lanky and white-faced behind the counter, his grey eyes bolting under his wild hair, as he stood "minding the shop" while our father was out back. In some mysterious way, the café, now, had changed colour. The ceiling was orange in the smoky light and everything else was warm brown, red, laughing faces and drum-hollow mouths. Fiddler Winter was there against the far wall. He laughed back at the people who laughed at him because he wanted to finish his supper. Money rattled in the till.

Fiddler, for once, was sitting with his back to the service door so that I could see the girl who sat opposite, smiling into his eyes. It was Mary Mond.

Mary was lovely, like a rose. In fact a rose was actually named after her. Yet there was an obvious lack of inhibition in her that announced that the roots of the rose were very deep in the earth. I remembered suddenly, having seen her at one of the political lectures that Michael Campbell had given in Camden Town. This was before I had begun to attend the talks on music at Westminster and before I had got to know the Monds. On meeting Mary in her own home it had not occurred to me that there was anything extraordinary in this. I had merely thought that the lectures were the kind that might be attended by anyone with more than average intelligence. Now I saw it all in a different light and became aware of something strangely exciting. Mary washed her hair every night, intuitively I knew that it was because she sat in our café every night. Mary, beautiful and cherished, was secretly in love with Fiddler Winter.

Winter was a Czechoslovakian Jew who worked as an economist and studied music. Economy was even now sometimes spelled with a diphthong. He and his mother, bereft, had left their native village and sought peace all over Europe and the Near East. He used to sing a song of crows who became gipsies, and, amongst his friends, it earned him the nickname of "Crex". I associated him, still, with that society to which Stella Jackson and Michael Campbell had given me a brief introduction. Eavesdropping on his conversation awakened nostalgic memories.

My mother clattered along the passage with a tray. "Go up to the babies!" she whispered urgently to me. Always we spoke in whispers when there were customers in the shop. I whispered back and strode swiftly up the stairs. As I went the violin keened, the singing started in the shop and one of the twins called out.

Pamela was sitting up in bed with the light on, looking into her own mouth in a mirror. She had seen a baby cry so that his uvula showed and, made recently aware of certain features of anatomy by a nasty little boy at school, was looking down her throat to see if she had one too.

It was a quarter-past one and the moon had clouded over. Through the silence came the sound of the till being cleared and the bolts being shot in the café door. The light out into the garden snapped back like a bit of elastic and I crept into the front room which was over the shop. There was a kind of recess below in which couples would stand at night. This was distasteful to me, yet I looked down from the window all the same.

The streets had a shuttered look and the sky a cold aluminium lustre which only lovers could find eloquent. The warm shape of the people standing below the window was for a long time silent and unmoving. I opened the window and they heard the latch.

"It's all right," said Mary, "they're shutting the shop."

The man spoke: "It is the one thing over which I cannot help you. They are your parents. They will be hurt if they are made to feel that you could not tell them yourself. It would seem as though I came between them and you."

"I am afraid," said Mary Mond, "not of telling them, but of what they may do when they know. I couldn't bear to lose you now."

"My mother will not like it either. Her life has been hard, with no abiding place. She has no one else in the world." His strange English seemed to increase the gravity of his manner.

They talked with long pauses between sentences as though their thoughts overflowed.

"I am a wanderer. I have several languages and not one that I speak as a native. I have no native language. As soon as I open my mouth they think: 'Damn foreigner!' The English do not like foreigners and nobody likes a Jew."

"When I marry you then I shall be a damned foreigner. I'll be a Jew too."

Crex laughed. The girl went on: "I hate the coldness and the furtiveness of all this. Crex, couldn't we?"

There were times when the earthiness of the rose was an embarrassment to him. His voice was very gentle: "Then we should need to be more furtive than ever."

"But at least we should know each other. That would be something nobody could take away."

His arm was loose about her and they were both silent in the uncompromising quiet of the street. At last he said: "I do not want to harm you. I think it might damage both of us but you much more than me."

Mary moved suddenly from his loosened embrace. She looked very young and straight, like a sheltered sapling and her eyes were visible from above so wide were they with incredulity. Her voice had a timbre like the note of a tall-stemmed glass when the rim is rubbed with wine. She sounded, all at once, very like Nicola. "Do you mean you refuse?"

There was a world of tenderness in his voice: "I should not dream of refusing."

The Mond house seemed hardly like a town house at all. Lying on the lawn with Nicola, one could look dreamily about and reflect that this might be a secluded garden anywhere. There was the scent of roses and old trees, yew, cypress, cedar and bay. There were the terraced lawns, the shrubbery and the pond. Only if one listened very intently could one hear the sound of traffic in the far distance. Then that sound too was masked by the hum of a plane which described a vast parabola against the smooth sky.

I stared at Nicola. I felt that I should never get tired of looking at her. Nicola's hair was rattan gold and her neat plaits hung below her waist like two jointed yellow ivory snakes. The plaits began on the top of her head and her own meticulous little fingers gathered the strands of her hair from temple, crown and brow and with delicate strong movements of her hands, with graceful movements of her slender arms, she twisted and smoothed her long hair until each strand was part of the delicious pattern. So beautifully was it done that, in repose, the whole of her head and perfect face seemed like a Chinese carving.

I had a strong desire to be in some way superior to this perfect thing that was Nicola. I knew something that she did not. I said: "I know why Mary washes her hair every night."

Unwillingly Nicola was impressed and I continued to be

mysterious until Nicola said with dramatic intensity: "If you don't tell me I'll never speak to you again!"

For a moment I felt deflated, but the feeling of importance returned when Nicola drew in her breath sharply and bit her lip.

Mrs. Mond came out with a lady. Otis followed closely. The lady was a Mrs. Forth. She said pleasantly to me: "You play the piano, don't you?" It was obvious that, to Mrs. Forth, "being musical" meant nothing but that.

"No," I answered, "hardly at all. Ours is no good, you see, so I couldn't practise."

"Angela understands music," said Otis. "Either you know about it or you don't and Angela just does."

"She ought to be able to play," Nicola chimed in a voice like a Cox's Orange Pippin, "her fingers are so long."

Mrs. Forth smiled. "You have nice hands," she said, trying hard.

I knew this to be true. It seemed to me that my hands were the only things about me that were good, but people did not notice them.

Nicola said: "Your fingers are bow-legged."

Everybody laughed. That was witty of Nicola for the boneless look about my hands was due partly to the fact that my fingers were all curved. I felt ill-at-ease again.

We went upstairs together for Nicola to change for the concert. In this wonderful house Nicola had not a bedroom to herself but a little suite of rooms. When one had closed the door that led from the balcony one was in what I thought of as a self-contained flat with a little hall of its own.

While Nicola was dressing there was a faint rustle in the small carpeted hall, and when we came out of the bedroom I could see that the bathroom floor had been repolished, the towels renewed and the pale peach-coloured bath become miraculously clean and dry again. As we went down the stairs Nicola's dress was a parachute of thick cream shantung.

"Otis likes you," said Nicola, pertly. "He always likes girls with long hair."

I felt suddenly self-conscious about my tumble of very ordinary brown hair. I wore it in two bunches, tied with green ribbons which I kept as crisp as I could by wetting them at night and leaving them wound round the bed-rail till morning.

"You ought to have your hair cut short."

"Why?"

"Because Otis will probably fall in love with you for your hair alone. If you have it cut and he still likes you then you'll know that he loves you for yourself and not for your hair."

We put on our coats and went out to the car which Dr. Mond had driven round to the front door.

I felt worried about my hair.

When we were sitting in the back of the car Dr. Mond said kindly: "Angela will need a rug coming back; her coat's not very thick."

"Isn't it? I always feel all right."

Dr. Mond merely smiled and I felt creeping over me that old sensation which had so paralysed me at the sight of the service lift at the Waterton's house. I felt that my clothes were lined with sandpaper and all the nerves in my body were on edge, like teeth.

The feeling did not leave me in the concert hall. I was in that mood when everything remembered was a past humiliation. Even as I sat on the plush seat I was reminded of the first time I had ever entered a theatre of any kind. I had not expected the seat to tip up and, after adjusting my coat, had sat down ignominiously on the floor; then I had made it worse by remarking to a friend who, I thought, was about to do the same: "The seats tip up, you know," and all the people who had refrained from laughing at first, laughed then.

I began to play with a little scar on my forefinger. This scar I had given to myself with an ordinary Gillette razor blade. I found it on the dresser at home and did not know what it was. My father had, until then, always used a "cut-throat". The razor blade looked as though it would be sharp and I "tried" it on my finger.

A fair and very young man came on to the stage with a violin. When he began to play, people whispered: "He is nervous!" "Look how nervous he is!"

I was glad that at last there was another whose happiness was, perhaps, as precarious as my own, and I remarked to

109

no one in particular: "Yes, he is nervous; his left hand is trembling."

Fatefully the music stopped just in time for Nicola to giggle and say in a pig's whisper: "Ass! That's not nerves, that's tremolo. He does it on purpose."

I shrank into my seat. A draught blew in and chilled my body while my cheeks burned. And Nicola was wrong! I knew then suddenly what I should have known before. I looked round wildly. I wanted to say to all the people who regarded me with compassion: "Of course I know and Nicola doesn't. I just wasn't thinking."

The lovely Mary leaned forward from behind and whispered: "I know. Don't say anything," and I turned to meet her smile and felt like Judas.

Mrs. Forth smiled at me and Otis looked over Nicola's head and tried to catch my eye but I avoided it. I understood consciously for the first time that lack of sensitivity in Nicola that took her so easily through life.

The violin sobbed again. In such a mood all music seemed to me to be inexpressibly mournful.

Going back in the car Otis said: "Angela is the best in our musicianship class. She learns pieces from the score and plays them from memory without any effort at all."

"That sounds very clever," answered Mrs. Forth.

"But I only do it with simple pieces and the melody is easy."

"Oh, I can do that, but not the harmony that Angela can do."

"Well," I answered confident that anything I might say would be readily understood by everyone in such a highly-educated group of people, "there is a limited number of things which you can expect a chord to do. If it does what you expect, then it's easy to remember; if it does something else, you're so surprised you can't forget."

Dr. Mond nearly forgot that he was driving and flung back his head in laughter so that Mrs. Mond remarked: "Darling, we'd all like to live to hear Angela make an explanation like that another day."

The Monds left me not far from the café. Dr. Mond offered to take me all the way home but I said that I liked to walk and was surprised, on thinking it over, to find that that was true.

So the change from the atmosphere surrounding the Mond family to the acrid sweat and clatter, smoky, cut-it-with-a-knife atmosphere of the café need not be too sudden.

I was nearly home. The nausea slipped from me like a hair shirt. I took deep breaths of air and smoke and exhaust gas and began to walk more easily. I wanted some tea and I wanted it from the china ladle bowl which I always used as a cup at home. I had found it on a rubbish dump in the Ellington Street days, a blue and white china ladle, broken so that only an inch of the handle remained. It had been my "cup" ever since, for I preferred it to the thick white café cups of which there were now so many.

Sitting in the hot kitchen, sipping tea, I said to my mother: "May I have my hair cut?"

My mother merely said: "I suppose that means you've got it in a tangle again."

I felt relieved. I could not have my hair cut; my mother would not let me.

In the darkness that night I spread my hair over the pillow. Otis liked my hair. I knew that in many ways I was "different" and this was not altogether good, but, at least, I was ordinary to look at.

I had opened the front room window earlier in the evening. When the café closed, I went and looked down into the street. Two people stood there as the quiet congealed them. It was the kind of warm night on which the senses are assailed; touch burns, cries in the night form like cracks in the dry earth and odours are intensified. But the lovers stood as though numbed by the very depth of their feeling. Crex wore a heavy mackintosh, stiff as a board and grimed with the soot of years.

"What are we going to do?"

"Robert has given me the key of his flat. He is away for the rest of the week."

Her voice was startled as she said: "Does he know why you wanted it?"

"I did not tell him." I could see, from above, his long Jewish face. He stretched an arm to lean on our window and his hot hands slipped on the glass. His raincoat grumbled like a dead sail and the stale smell of rubber seemed to come from it in little gusts. His raincoat thrust out reptilian points at mad angles and the girl stood, arrested, in dismay.

"Crex, let's not, not now." I could hear them breathing. "I'm going to go."

They stood on the pavement and kissed apart, the raincoat between them. When Mary had gone I still waited to see what Crex would do. He was swearing in a grunting fashion, as though each word were knocked out of him by a blow in the solar plexus. Suddenly he ripped off his raincoat and flung it on the ground. He leaned his forehead on the window-pane and the sounds that came from him were wordless. I did not want to watch any more.

Although, from this time the friendship between Nicola and me weakened and, eventually, came to an end, yet my visits to the Mond house surprisingly did not cease. It was not arithmetic now but musicianship, and Otis insisted that I be invited.

Thus it came about that I found myself there one Saturday afternoon when Nicola was out and Mrs. Mond took me up to her own bathroom. This too was in a suite set apart with a bedroom, a dressing-room and a study. I had been here before but I had never been left here alone really to commune. I laid a cheek against the satin wall of the bedroom. It was of the gentlest yellow, paling to sun-cloud white, the colours of the rose called "Peace".

I went across into the bathroom. Mrs. Mond had told me not to hurry and I was delighted with this allowance of time. There were red and white striped curtains at the windows and round a shower, and there was a strange low thing near the towel rail. It looked as though it ought to be sat on, so I sat on it. There were two taps of the kind that are pressed. I leaned on them with my hands. They were not stiff, as I had thought, and the next moment I stood up, drenched.

There was a scarlet towel on a rail, a shaving towel, I thought, and I squeezed on it as much of my wet clothes as I could. The navy blue dye came out and left distinct dark patches on the red. There were little puddles of water on the shining black floor.

At last I went downstairs again with misery in my gait and a feeling of panic. During tea I balanced on my coccyx on the edge of a little chair so awkwardly that people must have thought I was in pain. I felt stupefied with discomfort.

Then, from the study, we heard the voice of Octavius Mond. Mrs. Mond went into the hall and I followed. Nicola was there already.

"And who is this Winter, this Crex, this—crow?"

Octavius Mond was Nicola's grandfather and, although he lived in his son's house, was rarely seen. Yet in times of crisis his word was unquestioned, or almost unquestioned. As a last resort, in family discussion he would fall back upon his religion and this invariably had the effect of so embarrassing the rest of the family that they could not argue.

"Has he no other name?"

Mary's soft voice answered: "Hezron, Bezaleel, Ephraim."

"Are those Christian names?"

"No. He's a Jew."

"A Jew."

Octavius, who had paced over to the corner of the room now turned and faced his granddaughter. His height was considerable. He was the kind of man who rarely fails to develop a stoop, in middle age, if only to protect his head. As it was, his back was like a wall, for, in Octavius's life, door-frames and ceilings had always been made high enough for him.

"Have you forgotten what they did to our Lord?"

Nicola, from the doorway, whispered: "Crex had got an alibi. He wasn't born then."

But Octavius heard her. He stopped speaking and I felt that the eyes of this family were turned not on Nicola but on me. In some way they seemed to feel that I was to blame for the whole disreputable business.

"The children had better go."

But Mary's words followed us: "I have not forgotten what He said from the cross."

I wish I had dared to turn and look at the face of Octavius. At that moment he must have known that his granddaughter was going to defy him in a way that his children had, apparently, never done.

Otis said to me: "Let's try to play *The Midsummer Night's Dream* duets."

Then my stupefaction gave place to fright and a last passionate urge to win back some semblance of normality. I must not, I could not sit on the piano stool. Almost against my will my voice rose in a high imitation of Nicola in a dominating mood.

"Oh, I can't play. Listen! There's a wonderful film on at the Everyman. We've simply got to see it. Come on! Oh, come on!"

Otis gave a message to the maid, for his mother was speaking on the telephone as we left and, for once, I was insistent.

It was a revival of *Dr. Caligari*, and we sat for an hour watching the antic mouthings of the characters in the old silent film. Given another five or six years I might have viewed it with some sophistication, would have pointed out that it was a "classic" and something that everybody saw, at least once. Now, it seemed merely grotesque, like the whole situation, and I itched and fidgeted with warmth and my wet clothes. When I said good-bye to Otis outside the cinema I knew I could never visit the Monds again.

I was young and molehills throw long shadows in the morning. On the way home from the cinema I sat in the heat of the empty train, staring at the cabled walls of the "Tube" which seemed to symbolise the life before me, tortuous and grey. The strain of the afternoon overwhelmed me and I found myself sobbing, deeply and silently. I felt like a wind-pump, a heaving diaphragm that sobbed with the whirring wheel of the sails and the wheel, set in motion by regret, was a kaleidoscope of pictures, a quiet garden, roses, peace and satin walls. But, even in that moment, I had a misgiving. Nicola would not have thought in that way. To be conscious of my diaphragm when my world was shattered! And Nicola would never have been struck by any tragedy so humiliatingly comic.

I supposed it would remain a secret to the end of my days, a secret almost too awful to think about, yet even then I had a distant hope that, years ahead, I might again know someone with whom I could be so completely myself that I could share it.

A different tremor passed through me. I caught sight of my reflection in the opposite window. One of the notable things about a school panama was the ease with which it went out of shape, especially in the rain. The crown, gently convex, by design, tended to work itself up to form a point and the brim drooped. The whole thing became conical, resembling nothing so much as a clown's hat three times enlarged. As I looked at the image in the opposite window, the lips twitched. Well, I couldn't help it. The reflection grinned back at me, a squirming schoolgirl in a funny hat. What was the use of having won a scholarship; what was the use being clever if you could not tell when the vibrato came from the diaphragm and not the heart?

# CHAPTER VIII

## *FISH AND CHIPS AND DISILLUSION*

THE Fore Street café was probably a newer building than any we had previously occupied. All the doors were smaller and there was a great deal of yellow varnish about, but we had electric light. Nearly everyone I knew had electricity in their houses. We were the only ones who, until now, had had the business of going into rooms in the dark, groping for matches, feeling for the gas tap, and achieving, after a minor explosion, an aggressive roar and a roomful of white light. The gas "mantles" which became white-hot were as flimsy as snowflakes and constantly needed to be renewed. All the same the hum of gas lighting and the singing of the kettle on the kitchen range had always seemed to me to be the inevitable concomitant of warm winter evenings. It was wonderful to have electric light, nevertheless; without doubt it was a decided advance.

There was the café itself in the front of the house, a large room with composition floor and tiled tables. One could go straight through the café to the yard at the back. (It was vulgar to call it a yard, refined to call it a "garden", which it was not.) Out through the "shop" was the back door into the kitchen and another door which was that of the outside lavatory that male customers were supposed to use. The kitchen here was never a place of peace and comfort. On one side of it the range, which was in use perpetually, made everything too hot. On the other side there was a draught from the door leading into the yard. The kitchen was too small for it to be possible to get away from either of these discomforts, and it was, besides, nearly always full of café cooking and sometimes even the café washing-up. There was nothing labour-saving about any of it. My mother cooked in the way she had always cooked for the family. She made all the cakes. And we washed up in the ordinary way of washing-up, with one person to "wash" and another to "dry" on tea-towels that, in their turn, had to be washed by hand. My brother and I did our homework in all the hot and cold, fuss and bustle of this kitchen. Often, after the "pubs" had closed, a party of people would come in and stay until about one o'clock. They would sing and play mouth-organs, accordions and Crex Winter's violin. It was impossible for any of us to sleep until they went.

One night they were rowdier than usual. My brother and my father were out there. But, from the kitchen, we could hear dancing and raucous laughter. A chair was knocked over. My mother grew alarmed, but she could not leave her cooking. She told me to peep through the door and see what was happening. I did this and saw my father, with his apron rolled up, tap-dancing all round the café and making as much noise as anyone.

There was a row about this afterwards. My mother was disgusted, angry and bitter and my six-year-old sister Pamela said it was disgraceful. Daphne grinned and herself practised tap-dancing more assiduously than ever, until my mother put a stop to it. And I, in spite of the fact that I was more "refined" than anyone in the family, could not help feeling that it was all rather fun. There seemed to be no sense in running a café if you could not enjoy it. Why shouldn't we dance and sing in the intervals between washing up and pouring cups of tea?

In the summer we made ice-cream. On the whole I had little to do with any of the work connected with the café. Mostly I looked after my sisters. My mother made the ice-cream mixture and my father and my brother did the work of "freezing" it. The mixture was put into a cylindrical container which was placed in a still larger container and packed round with ice and saltpetre. My brother would sit on a stool in the garden, holding this apparatus between his knees and swinging round the inside vessel until the ice-cream became solid. It seemed rather like making butter in an old-fashioned churn. There was a sweet-shop down the road that also sold ice-cream and my sisters spread the story that the boy who served it used to clean his utensils by licking them.

My bedroom was immediately above the kitchen. The house had been built with living accommodation upstairs which could be quite apart from the downstairs premises, although we never used it in this way, and my room had an outside door from which steps led into the garden. There was a sink in my bedroom, a large rectangular kitchen sink, with a draining-board, but there was no cooker. Next to my bedroom was a bathroom, the first we had ever had. Brooms and mops were piled in the corner. The other two rooms on this floor were my parents' bedroom and the front room, but the latter was hardly used; we could not afford to heat it and, since the café was open about eighteen hours out of twenty-four, we had no leisure anyway.

The top floor was let, except for one small room in which my brother slept. To begin with we let unfurnished to a family. I cannot remember how many children they had but they seemed numberless. They were all very dark and attractive, like gipsies, and they ran noisily up and down all day and half the night. Judging from the snatches of shouted conversation that came down to us, they had no set times for meals, but each one's "rations" were left out for them to take when they chose. They did not stay long and when they went, we found the place swarming with bugs and hopping mad with fleas.

Our next tenants were a mother and her little girl, Maureen. The father was away, I think in the Navy. Maureen was very pale and her mother dressed her in buttercup yellow. The effect was unfortunate. She was a little younger than my sisters, who used to take her to school between them. When she developed measles my sisters brought her home and, a fortnight later, they too had got measles. They were very ill indeed. My mother was busy with the café. I had had measles and would not be infected again. The children lay there in the darkened room with their eyes swollen and running, their little faces flushed with the savage fever. It was one of the most harrowing experiences of my life, looking after them.

After this, my parents decided to let the spare rooms furnished. I hardly ever went up to the top of the house but I have an idea that the "furniture" consisted of little more than two or three iron bedsteads.

The people who took these rooms were all men and I can recall only one of them. His name was "Jock" and I remember him best on the day that he left us, having lost his job. He came into our kitchen, sat in my father's chair, took one of my sisters on his knee and started to sing *I belong to Glasgow*. He was going back there that day. He was in exaggeratedly high spirits and soon we were all singing with him, and the kitchen was nearly as noisy as the café at night.

After he had gone my father said that he had not paid his rent and my father was almost sure that now he never would. My mother was bitterly angry. Why had my father done nothing about it? Since he knew what was happening, why had he not got in touch with the police? My father made the noise of disgust which (in spite of our "superiority") he always made at the mention of police or prison warders, and said one couldn't do a thing like that. Then I remembered that my father had sung and laughed as loudly as any of us.

Financially the café was failing fast. My father was irritable and wiry and strong enough not to be afraid of anyone, yet he had given poor, guilty little Jock as happy a "send-off" as he could. I had a feeling that my father's standards of behaviour were probably the highest I should ever know.

There was always a good deal of food about now, but most of it was not for us. I remember once going into the kitchen and asking for one of the rock-cakes that my mother had made. I was told I could not have one; they were for the shop. I was hungry and sick of soft bread. The cakes were only a penny each. I was allowed a shilling a week pocket money, although there were times when I did not get it. I went out into the café, sat at a table, slapped my shilling on the table and ordered a dozen rock-cakes.

The scar looked white on my father's lip. He told me to go back into the kitchen and I did. He said that as long as there was food in the house his children should have it. He set the cakes in front of me and told me to take what I wanted. By then I did not want any of them, but I ate one. I thought my father would have murdered me if I had not.

My shilling a week was less than most people at school were given and I resented this. When I got nothing at all I resented it more than ever. My father would say:

"Not just at the moment," and he would continue to say this until the end of another week. It annoyed me, because all he had to do was to open the drawer of the till and give me a shilling out of it. Once, when there was a book I very much wanted on the second-hand bookstall I decided to take my shilling and tell my father about it afterwards, but when I opened the drawer of the till I found it empty. I never asked again.

It was for the sake of my sisters that I began to go to church. I felt that to go was part of their education and I marched them off one Sunday morning just before eleven. They could not read sufficiently well to follow the service, but they wanted the place found in their prayer-books and hymn-books. One hymn went on and on. At the end of each verse there was a pause, then another verse began. After the eighth verse Pamela thought the hymn must end and her little voice rang out very high and clear in a long-drawn-out "Amen". Everyone in front turned round. My sisters were very small. Only I was visible above the backs of the high pews. The church was St. Luke's, not far along the road from our home. The vicar spoke to us afterwards and he came to see us at the café. He was a ponderously fat man with a big ragged moustache. I started attending Sunday school again, not now to drop halfpennies into an umbrella, but as a teacher, although it seemed peculiarly incongruous that I should do this wearing my school hat; I had no other.

The vicar of St. Luke's was an extraordinary person and immensely popular not only in his own parish but with people from the neighbouring one of St. John's. Our vicar was nick-named "Old Bill". Everyone called him that, but his name was Kelly. He had nothing to recommend him. He was a bachelor and the vicarage lacked, conspicuously, any feminine touch. He was so big that he could hardly get about. Under his small, round ridiculous little hat his little eyes gently watered in the folds of his vast pale face which was decorated by a moustache like a feather boa. The swelling fronts of his waistcoat were not clean. I never saw him eat but he blew and snuffled as he talked. He was tall and when he walked shuffled and swayed like an elephant on its hind legs. But he trumpeted into the lives of everyone he met and he brought regularly to his church people who other-wise would never have seen the inside of it, except for christen-ings, weddings and funerals. He saw that I was introduced to other members of the congregation who were my age and I attended the socials and dances and concerts that Old Bill was always getting people to organise.

Most of the young people there attended the Latimer School in Haslebury Road and most of them, also, really belonged to the parish of St. John's on the east side of the main road. After church we used to go for walks eastwards along the North Circular Road to where the New River flowed round the gasworks. Here the river looked much more as I thought it should, for it flowed through waste land and its banks were grassy.

The matter of confirmation came up. Sonia had been confirmed in St. Paul's Cathedral. I had known about it, at the time, but guessed that it was not for me. Nearly everyone I knew had been christened, hardly anyone had been confirmed. Nobody seemed to think it was incongruous that I should nevertheless have been made godmother to my sisters. Now, when Mr. Kelly started his new confirmation class, I joined with the others of my age.

After I was confirmed I became passionately religious. I attended every service that I could and entered into long discussions with Kylo at school. I tried to do the same with Old Bill but he was, in some ways, too clever for me. He was sincere and even earnest just as long as I was, but he seemed to know instantly when I became pretentious and began to talk merely for the sake of exercising my ideas, and his long face would split right across and his watery eyes would run. He would let out a snirt of laughter that splayed his moustache and raise his stick to push me away from him with the end of it.

Some of the teaching staff at school had come to realise that it was impossible for me to study adequately at home. It was arranged that I should remain in school every evening, for an hour or two, and do my homework then. I was given tea which a maid brought into the classroom on a tray. It was daintily set out with an embroidered tray cloth and the bread and butter was almost as thin as the china. People were really too kind.

There was another girl in the form whose home background was nearly as difficult as my own. She lived somewhere between Seven Sisters Road and Holloway Road. Her name was Margery Denotkin. Her father was Polish and her mother had been Scottish. She died and Mr. Denotkin married again a woman who presented him with a new young family and with whom Margery was perpetually at loggerheads. After a while similar facilities were offered to her so that each evening after school we had our tea and sat in the form-room together. It was natural that we should talk all the time and do no work at all. On some evenings I went home with her; on some, neither of us went home at all, until very late, but spent the evening walking about and talking. This was very different from the way in which Sonia and I had indulged in the same pastime. Margery knew numbers of people who had left school and were working. She knew young people of both sexes. We used to meet them when they left work and then stand around leaning against shop windows or, when it rained, lolling under the railway arches in the Seven Sisters Road. Margery was friendly with an errand boy named Ernie, but he told us, in confidence, that really, he was not an errand boy at all but a member of the Secret Service. One of the girls in this group of friends went away to have an illegitimate baby and that frightened us. She was a pretty, gentle girl and we felt that if this could "happen" to her then it might happen to anyone.

The fancy garters had gone out of fashion. It did not occur to me as I stood, leaning against the brickwork, with a group of girls in tight skirts slit from the hem to an inch above the knee and their transparent "art" silk blouses that they were not unlike the fish and chip brigade which had frightened me so in my extreme youth, and it did not occur to me either that, in spite of the fact that my clothes hardly conformed, I was now one of them.

But even in the matter of clothes and hair I managed fairly well, by these standards. Next door to the café was a hairdresser's shop. It was run by a Jewish family called "Owide" and they had "Maison Owide" in gold lettering over their window. My hair was naturally curly and the eldest son used to "borrow" me to demonstrate new styles on and to try out his new assistants. I had a feeling that he sometimes "borrowed" me when he did not really need me at all. His sister was a volatile blonde, taller than I. She had a vivid taste in clothes and used to give me things she had grown tired of. These, altered by me and worn with my only pair of school shoes, must have looked remarkable.

At the same time I became interested in the writings of Sir Walter Scott and on many evenings I sat in the Edmonton public library, reading Trevelyan's work on him. I never stopped writing verse.

When I was fourteen I took jobs during the school holidays. In those days it was an unusual thing to do and the whole business seemed to me to be cheap and nasty. For one thing I knew that, at school, it would be regarded seriously and unfavourably. For another I never told prospective employers that I did not intend to remain. I merely applied for a job at the beginning of the holiday and gave notice a week before the end. I did clerical work in large firms where employees were always coming and going. The work was repetitive and deadly and the outlook completely different from that at school. Outside we were the least important beings in the world. Sometimes, during notices, after prayers, Kylo would give a talk on what employers required from girls and how we should dress for interviews, and I used to sit and listen and want to howl at the irony of it all. At school we were individuals, yet somebody would notice if a house badge was missing; at work we were automatons and nobody cared how we looked. I could have told her that nobody wanted initiative, intelligence was no asset, and provided work was done with a modicum of accuracy, nobody cared what you thought of it. I could have told her of the hush that fell one minute before the electric clock gave the time for leaving and the panic rush, the shrilling voices and the thundering feet, a minute later. The ages of our school teaching staff probably averaged half a century, but into our way of living they had not even been born.

I felt that the best part of my life was over. All that I valued was gone, Sonia, the Watertons, the Monds, art and music. I was in a different world now and the gulf was wide. Only literature remained and this I cherished alone. Even from St. Luke's Church most of the people whom I knew had gone, for there was a new vicar at St. John's and Old Bill, from the pulpit, had asked his parishioners to give their support, so they transferred their allegiance. Old Bill himself, soon after, stood on the edge of a grave which subsided so that he fell in, and he did not long survive this accident.

Sometimes, after school, when my group of acquaintances in the Seven Sisters Road were not available, and I did not want to go home, I would walk round the shops, mostly miscellaneous stores and department stores. I would go round these shops in the way that I had once wandered round museums and art galleries, just gazing and getting a kind of spiritual stimulation from it. I needed food for dreams and found it here and found, too, that it made the whole of life more tolerable.

One day, when I left the shops and began to dawdle home, I had in my pocket a rather small white and gold cardboard box. In it was a tiny bottle of pale-pink nail varnish, cuticle oil, varnish remover, orange sticks and emery board. The value of the whole thing was probably about three shillings and six-pence. I had always been vain about my hands. I varnished my nails at night and lay on my bed, watching them twinkle. They looked like wet shells tossed by spray into the sunshine. My hands might have belonged to the most privileged woman in the world. But I had to take off the varnish before morning. During the term I was not able to explain how I had come by it; only when I was in a holiday job was I able to tell my parents that a friend at work had given it to me.

There are at least two ways of stealing. The first arises from the desperate need of concrete things, like food or fuel, and one steals directly the thing that one needs. But the conflict between one's moral feelings and the impulse to steal is very great. It is hard to be anti-social when one does not feel like it and I have never been able to do this; the anxiety is intolerable.

The second arises in a different way and is much easier to carry out. There is a feeling that the whole of one's life is un-satisfactory and that one is wholly outside one's own element; by temperament, ability and inclination one belongs in a certain sphere and only circumstance has kept one out of it. There is no very great gap between "I belong to all this" and "This belongs to me". The transition is not difficult. One cannot appro-priate to oneself a sphere of life, only something which one thinks of as a symbol of that, and the "symbol", once possessed, very soon ceases to be symbolic, so that the whole business must be gone through again. One does not need the thing that one steals; one may not even want it. One's moral susceptibilities cease to function. It does not feel like stealing because what one takes is already regarded as one's own and there is no conflict. None of all this is at all logical; it is just the way things sometimes happen.

Donald Soper, at the Islington Central Hall, was running a canteen for the unemployed. Margery Denotkin and I wanted to help and went to see him. He said he would like us to serve in his canteen provided our parents knew all about it. They did not. When I told my father he was furious. He said that the men who went there were the scum of the earth and no daughter of his was going to serve teas to them. He said all the things about the unemployed that everyone else had been saying for years.

One day, at school, I left my own money in the pocket of my coat in the cloakroom. This we were not allowed to do, so that, when I reported that my money had gone, I got little sympathy, although everybody made a fuss. I did not tell my parents.

Officially the thief was never discovered, but after the fuss had died down I remembered several small incidents that seemed to be related. The cloakrooms normally were locked at nine and only a small number of people had permission to enter them at irregular times. Also it seemed unlikely that anyone should have gone round feeling in all the pockets; it seemed much more probable that it was somebody who knew me and knew my habit of leaving money in my coat. I had decided too that it must be one of the obviously deprived people who were developing along lines that I had begun to know. There was only one girl who came into all of these categories, and, as I was ruefully counting the few coppers that I had left, I saw her looking at me and our eyes met. She said: "I have a feeling that you think I took your money."

I said that I did think so, and she immediately burst into tears. So did I, and we sat on the bench in the cloakroom quietly crying and not looking at one another.

The incident brought about a change in me and I never again stole in the same way. I can imagine some moralists saying, with triumph, that the reason was obvious. All I needed was a taste of my own medicine to make me realise what it was like to be victimised. But the feeling was not like that at all. It was simply that I suddenly regarded myself in a different light. I was placed in a different category. I no longer felt deprived and envious. I was the kind of person who was stolen from. This other girl had given me what I needed, as surely as though she had handed me a fortune on a plate.

I did not even miss the money seriously. It meant merely that I walked home for the next four nights, and I liked walking, because I could dream, from Blackstock Road all the length of the Seven Sisters Road and along the High Road, Tottenham. It did not take any longer and was not much more tiring than standing around with Margery Denotkin.

Some weeks later, as I was walking down Blackstock Road, I saw Sonia standing at the window of a pet shop. She was watching some kittens. Sonia liked animals much more than I did, for I had the babies. We grinned at each other rather self-consciously. We had not spoken to each other for some months. Sonia said that their large cat, "Boz", had died and she thought she would buy a kitten. We left the shop giggling, Sonia with the little cat wrapped in her school scarf and I carrying both our cases.

Sonia said she could not get the kitten home by herself and would I come with her. I wondered what Sonia's mother would think about this, but Sonia said that her mother was away and only her grandmother was in the house. We told the grandmother that my name was "Ethel". Grandma had aged a good deal and was rather blind now. She thought she had seen me before and we agreed that she had. She spent some time trying to remember which Ethel I was. We called the cat Balthazar. Thereafter Sonia and I were together again and when I took a job the next holiday she met me every evening as I left work.

After I had been five years at the high school it was decided that I should leave. I found the usual dull routine job at the end of the summer term but I went into this one, knowing that my parents wanted nothing so much as that I should remain in it for the rest of my life.

I felt physically ill and I looked it. My face was so white and my eyes so dark that people remarked on it. I was probably anæmic. I was certainly tired, so tired that each evening I did nothing at all but sit in a chair until it was time to go to bed.

My mother had had everything beautifully planned. I should take a clerical job, which was nice and clean and superior, with comparatively high pay and comparatively short hours, and everything that I wanted to do with my life could be fitted into my spare time; see? And my refusal to "see" was the sole cause of things not fitting into this pattern at all.

From this first "permanent" job I did get a legitimate reprieve. Before I left school I had sat for an examination into the Civil Service, but the results had not come through by the end of term. They did so by about the end of the school holiday. I had fulfilled my mother's main ambition for me. I had succeeded in entering the Civil Service.

I was not due to report there for some weeks, but I at once demanded to leave the job I was in and which I hated. If my mother had said I must keep the job because we needed the money so badly, I could have understood, and I think I should not have resented it, but what she said was that I could leave it if I liked, but, if I did so, I must go back to school; I could not remain at home doing nothing. I had had no holiday that year and I badly needed time to myself, days and days of it in which to read and write in the library. My mother made it clear that this was a luxury I could not hope to have again, so, when the term started I reappeared at school.

Kylo greeted me as though I were a stranger and asked me why I had come. She thought I had left. She made it clear that I was not in the least welcome. I wanted to ask her if I could not sit in the school library, where I would not bother anyone, but I felt too depressed by it all. Instead I sat in my old form, with girls a year junior to me, and waited for the weeks to go, although the passing of time brought nearer my entry into the Civil Service which, through previous experience, I dreaded. Sonia had left. Those of my contemporaries who remained had gone into the sixth form. It was a time of infinite sadness.

The café had failed. There was now no doubt about it. One evening there was a long and awe-inspiring session with the lady who had bought it. The café would have to be sold again and we should leave. I guessed that my parents had timed their admission of failure to coincide with my leaving school, because they did not want to interfere with my education.

We moved to Battersea. My mother had been brought up in Lambeth, her sisters lived in Brixton and Herne Hill and she considered South London more refined than North London, and Walnut Tree Walk and the New Cut unaccountably superior to Roman Way and the Caledonian Road. The Battersea house was very near to Clapham Common and not very far from Wandsworth Common. It was in Shelgate Road and was older and, to me, more attractive than any house we had lived in so far. It was small and rather cramped. My bedroom had a sloping ceiling, a dormer window and wallpaper that was hideously patterned with dark red lilies and fruits like pomegranates. To begin with I hated this wallpaper, until I found a way of using the ugliness of its design. I had never been able to have pictures that I liked and so refused to have any at all. One day I stuck a picture of Julian Huxley on the wall. I had long admired him for his intellect and quite liked his looks. The picture was no bigger than a penny and, so strong was the design on my wall-paper that, unless one knew where to look, it made the little picture inconspicuous to the point of being invisible. I began to collect these penny-sized portraits and to stick them un-obtrusively all over the walls. Shaw, the Huxleys, Marx, Walter de la Mare, Philip Gibbs, James Joyce. My taste was catholic.

Sonia was working in a bank, a branch of the same bank in which her father had worked before he was killed in the First World War. The most excellent thing about this bank was that women who left to marry and later needed to return to work were always re-employed by them. Sometimes I would meet Sonia at the bank, a tiny branch on the corner of Bread Street and Watling Street. The bank was destroyed by fire in the Second World War. It was an insanitary little place with rats in the basement. I used to ring the bell and go and sit inside on a mahogany bench while the wretched clerks went on and on try-ing to effect a balance with debit and credit. Occasionally I had to wait as long as an hour, an hour and a half, or two, and Sonia would eventually come out red-eyed and jerking with strain. The commercial world was, for us, pure purgatory.

Often we went to meet Michael and, now, there was no mention of Stella. Michael took us to political lectures. Sonia was seeing a good deal of him. Apart from literature, politics and psychology were my main interest now. I very soon found the public library on Lavender Hill and there set to work to read systematically through all of Freud's works. It was not as difficult as I anticipated. I was acquainted with much of it already and with the works of other psychologists. It was easy to think in this idiom. And, with Sonia and Michael and the people I met with them, the talk was all of capitalism (with the stress on the second syllable and the glottal stop following), vegetarianism (boiled corn and lumps of cheese), sex and pre-natal influences (though none of them liked children), and free love, no one apparently having heard the axiom that the great lover never really loves at all. It seemed to me that they missed the one great emotional experience. But they were very sincere.

At home I spent a good deal of time with my sisters. Their well-being and their education was the most important thing in the world. From Edmonton I had taken them on picnics to Epping Forest, for walks in Pymmes Park, and the waste land round the gasworks and parts of the New River. Now I took them on Clapham Common and on Wandsworth Common and into Battersea Park. They went about in the summer wearing nothing but a pair of swimming-trunks. Many children did this. I could not help comparing it with the flannel petticoats in which I had been dressed.

At first, in Battersea, I felt completely uprooted. There was nothing now with which I was familiar and I remember standing at my dormer window in the early hours of the morning, tears running down my face with the loneliness of it all.

When I had stood around in South Hornsey with Margery Denotkin and Ernie we had often discussed the difficulty of getting our writings typed before submitting them for publication. We thought it deplorable that in order to publish our work it was necessary to have either sufficient money to pay a typist or sufficient mechanical skill to type oneself, as well as having access to a typewriter. As a telegraphist in the Civil Service I learnt to touch type and that was all that came of my mother's ambition for me. I certainly did not despise it, for the difficulties connected with being a writer seemed, at that time, to be almost insuperable. This was a step, and quite a long step, towards what I wanted for myself.

# CHAPTER IX

# *REBELLION*

WE first reported for work in the Civil Service on a Saturday morning. This was a day of initiation only, and we left at about half-past twelve. As we were leaving the Supervisor remarked: "Make the most of this week-end. You won't get another one as long." This gave me a feeling of utter dismay.

On the Monday the sun shone brilliantly and light sparkled all over the Thames. It was early autumn, the time of the year when people remark that the evenings are "drawing in". I knew that by the time I left work that night it would be dusk. I arrived late. I very nearly did not arrive at all. I was wretched and my parents were unsympathetic. Nobody else had these absurd feelings. All I could say was that I did.

I continued to go for nearly six months, although I was nearly in tears each morning that I arrived. My performance in the mechanical work which we did all day was barely adequate. I could not understand why I felt utterly stupid when I knew so well that I was not. Sometimes at night I walked home. The river along the Victoria Embankment was wholly beautiful. I felt excited by the architectural sweep of the new County Hall and the blocked solidity of Shell-Mex House, especially when they were floodlit after dark. I could have wandered all day along that stretch of river. I looked at the seats along the Embankment. It seemed to me not at all extraordinary that some people should want to sleep there. It still seems æsthetically attractive. Sometimes I stood on Westminster Bridge and looked down into the water. Many evenings I walked the length of Lambeth Palace, the Albert Embankment and the Wandsworth Road. Usually I travelled on the twenty-six tram between Clapham Junction and Blackfriars Bridge.

My parents were cruelly disappointed when I left the Civil Service. They could not understand why I had not regarded it as a wonderful opportunity. For a time I did nothing, merely reading and writing in the public library as I had wanted to do. Then, since I loved children, it was suggested that I should work voluntarily in a day nursery.

I enjoyed this work more than anything I had ever done. I had no money and could contribute nothing at home, but I do not think my mother minded what I did, as long as I left home each morning and returned at night. She did not want me in the house all day. My brother had taken a job in the grocery department of a large store. I think he was as unhappy as I was. He would spend his evenings sitting and doing nothing and sometimes his eyes were full of tears.

The nursery in which I worked voluntarily was in Cambridge Road which runs off Battersea Bridge Road. One of the characteristics of these places is an almost obsessional standard of cleanliness. We scrubbed floors and rows of tiny lavatories and each night we washed dozens of little overalls and twice as many pairs of knickers. All the children were put into clean clothes as soon as they arrived. We bathed the older ones in large sinks. At night, just before they went home, they dressed again in their own clothes. This seemed completely to change their personality. With some of them, the clothes in which they arrived were so dirty that we washed and dried them all during the day, although this was not part of the service.

The Dickens's mother brought two children. Babies of working mothers were accepted from four weeks old. Harry Dickens was three years old and had fair straight hair and startling brown eyes. Baby Dickens's age was only a matter of weeks. Their clothes were usually revolting, actively and æsthetically. Harry's were so unprepossessing one morning that I washed them all and dried them in the boiler-room, rather than put him back into them that night, as dirty as they were. The sister laughed at me and said I did not know the Dickens family, but my favourite Harry looked lively and fresh and beautiful when his mother clasped him to her that night.

The next morning he arrived in a completely different set of thoroughly dirty clothes. Apparently he had a brother, only a little older, who went to school. If ever Harry was sent home clean, he arrived in his brother's clothes next morning in the hope, presumably, that they would be washed as well. But I laughed, too, when Sister did the same for Baby Dickens and had him "handed in" next day, wrapped in a filthy ticking bolster cover. We had children from the worst of the Battersea slums, but we also had them from the wealthier area around the Park.

The children were divided into three groups: the babies, under a year, the "intermediates" who were under two and promoted from babyhood when they could walk, and the "seniors" who were all over two years old and under five. The four-year-olds became quite responsible little people. It was always a shock, meeting one of them in the street, to see how small they were. One little girl, named Joan, was proud of being able to fetch a cup of tea, in the middle of the morning, for the nurses on duty. Once or twice somebody saw her taking a sip out of it, but nearly always the cup arrived and was fairly full. Only once she went off to the kitchen and failed to come back. We found her sitting under the stairs, having drunk all the tea.

At ten years old I had been proud of my "twin" pram. Now from the nursery we took children into Battersea Park in prams which held six toddlers, three each side, sitting facing each other.

At first I had gone to the nursery only in the mornings. Gradually I went more often and stayed longer and longer. In my spare time I knitted grey uniform jerseys and long grey woollen leggings. Once again I was "good with the children" and the matron in charge, Matron Sillence, asked me if I would not like to take up the work as a career.

I was happier in it than in anything else I had known outside school, but I did not feel dedicated. I worked because I liked it, but there was no inner compulsion nor outward compulsion that I could not withstand. I had sometimes worked long hours, but nothing like the hours put in by the young nurses there. They seemed hardly ever to be able to get away and, when they did, were too exhausted to do anything but sleep. The children were spotless and everything that came in for their use, from outside, even new things, was either washed or fumigated with sulphur candles down in the cellar, and yet the nurses sometimes went for two or three weeks without a bath, not for lack of facilities but for lack of time and energy. When they first came they were fresh and alert and eager. Soon all the spirit was washed out of them. Looking back, I realised that there was not one of them whom I had not seen reduced to tears from utter weariness. Matron Sillence was aware of this and gave them mornings in bed whenever she could, but the schedule had to be adhered to. They slept in small dormitories, were given their uniform, and their pay was nominal (about five shillings a week). If they were lucky their parents kept them in clothes. I cared deeply about the work; I could not have borne the life.

When we first moved to Battersea we had no cat. I cannot think how this happened, since we nearly always had at least one, and home was not home without it. One day I saw, in a newspaper shop, either in Webbs Road or Battersea Rise, an advertisement for a kitten. It was being given away which was what we wanted. All our cats had been strays or gifts; we never went to a pet shop.

The people in Keildon Road, who were giving away a kitten, were named Ingpen. I went round to see them. They were very friendly and we talked for quite a long time. There were two elderly sisters and a brother who was not much in evidence. I said that I had heard their name only once before; it was the name of somebody who wrote on the poet Robert Browning. The old ladies told me that that was Roger Ingpen, their brother, and that their sister had married Walter de la Mare. After this we got on very well. I told them that I wanted to write and they accepted this seriously. They were almost the only people who ever had. They offered to read some of my stories and, having done so, said that I certainly knew how to write, but that life was not all sordidness and depression and I should try to be more "uplifting". I called the kitten "Clim" after the hero in one of the Russian novels I was reading at the time.

My father had no job. We knew this now, but I do not think my sisters did. I had, for some time, ceased to be aware of the divisions in the little hierarchy that had seemed so important ten years previously, I felt I had nothing in common with any of these people anyway. But the twins, now, were very much aware of these social distinctions. In Shelgate Road we were "upstairs people" and had no garden; "downstairs people" were superior to us, but the quiet of the Battersea side streets, with their small gabled houses, was a distinct improvement on Fore

Street, and one which the children could appreciate. On the first day the twins explored into the next street and came back to say that there were trees there. We might be "upstairs people" now but at least we lived in a street that was next to a street that was really an avenue. We had a bathroom but, again, only cold water and no adequate means of heating it, so that, socially, the bathroom did not really count. Sometimes I used to heat water in buckets and bowls and kettles on top of the kitchen range and bath my sisters; the bathroom was never used otherwise.

One thing really blighted the move to Battersea for us children. One of us overheard our parents discussing the eviction of the people who had been there before us. We could not ask about this but, on the first day there, as we wandered through the echoing bare-boarded rooms, we thought about that family and wondered why they had been turned out. I think all four of us felt guilty. Their disaster was our dread. We felt heartbroken for them.

From the bathroom window we could see Battersea power station, three tall chimneys which periodically emitted plumes of white smoke with peristaltic bulges. These chimneys and the lock in Chelsea became symbols of life in Shelgate Road. Later a fourth chimney was erected.

My sisters went to school in Broomwood Road and came home to dinner each day, as nearly all children did then. The ones who were unable to do this, mostly those with working mothers, went to the town hall for soup.

As is common in London, we hardly knew the people downstairs. They had one little boy and we did not know him either. The father was a window-cleaner; with all his capital invested in a barrow, a ladder and a pail. They seemed quite well off. The window-cleaner eventually, perhaps guessing our plight, offered to take my father with him, so my father, now over sixty, started to clean windows.

He had another interest in Battersea and that was the Battersea running track. In his younger days he had been something of an athlete and he now went down to the track every day to train. He won numbers of races for veterans. He trained my brother, he trained my sisters; he nearly trained me. I enjoyed running, but not racing. I preferred running with somebody to running against them and I did not care whether I was able to win or not. The manœuvring which so many people practised in order to get a good handicap for a race later in the season, which they hoped to win, I found distasteful.

All the social life I had ever known, outside school, had come about through St. Luke's Church in Edmonton. The nearest church to where we lived in Battersea was St. Barnabas on the north side of the common and I went there.

I do not remember the name of the vicar. He never called on us. I think I hardly ever saw him. He was due to leave the parish soon, in any case. He was much younger than Old Bill, he was married and had a family, but he made practically no impression on us, and the wife of the new vicar, when he came, announced that they would not stay long, as they had never been in one place for more than two years. There was, however, a vigorous group of young people attached to this church and it was they who spoke to me. All of them belonged either to the Rovers or the Rangers. It seems incongruous now that these people should have wanted to go on being Boy Scouts and Girl Guides, for they were a much older group than the one I had known in Edmonton. The ages ranged from mine, which was still only sixteen, to nearly thirty. When it was proposed, in the Girl Guides Association, that there should be an upper age limit of twenty-one, there was dismay in our Ranger Company, for this would have made nearly all of its members ineligible. All the other activities which had meant so much at St. Luke's were missing here at St Barnabas's.

When we were young, my brother and I had been passionately interested in Scouting. As soon as we had been allowed to join the public library we read *Scouting for Boys*, and then read it again. We nearly knew it by heart. But we had never been allowed to join anything connected with the movement. My father said he objected to children being put into military uniform, but we always knew it was just one of the things that we should never be able to afford. Now it all suddenly seemed possible and the idea of going to camp was wildly exciting.

Things generally were better, in the material sense, than we younger ones could remember. The end of the depression had come, unobtrusively, and everyone talked of prosperity now. There was still some unemployment but not much amongst young people. It was fairly easy to slip in and out of a variety of clerical jobs.

One of the Rangers was also Brown Owl, and my sisters became Brownies. It was months before I could also afford a uniform for myself, but I attended all the meetings of the company. There was only one girl my age. She was seventeen, her name was Freda Hands and she was still at school studying, I believe, English literature. She wrote poetry and, although I was by now more interested in prose, we spent long hours walking the streets near Alfriston Road, where she lived, and discoursing until nearly midnight. Once we bought some chips and, as we walked along eating them we met the vicar and offered him a potato, which he took. We discussed theology with him. The whole incident seemed to have a daringly emancipated, intellectual flavour very far removed from that of the newspaper suppers under the arches in the Seven Sisters Road. There was also a shop in the Northcote Road where one could buy faggots and pease pudding. The faggots were nearly black and made of pig's blood, spices and all kinds of chopped pig meat; the pease pudding was difficult to eat with one's fingers because it was sticky and very hot.

By the time I was able to afford a Ranger uniform, another difficulty presented itself; I had become an agnostic. It was some of the Pauline aspects of Christianity that I had most difficulty in accepting and, because of this, I had doubts about all religion as I knew it, but I had not sufficient insight to understand this. A higher officer in the Girl Guide Movement offered to help and, after we had talked for a while, suggested earnestly that I was being influenced by "some pernicious book". I realised, at first with a feeling of frustration, then with one of amusement, that she had not even begun to understand what I was talking about. In the end I said I did not mind "making the promise" but that for me it might not mean quite what it was intended to mean.

Some of the places where we camped were very beautiful and among the best was Shere. My acquaintance with the country had been very slight indeed, but I loved it and the names of living things, the flowers and grasses, birds and trees. Some of the tests on such subjects seemed extraordinarily elementary. For me time spent in camp was utter bliss and a complete release.

Once, for a long week-end, some of us went with a party of Rovers to stay in a bungalow which belonged to Freda Hands's mother. The bungalow was on Pagham beach, near Bognor, and was constructed from railway carriages set to make three sides of a square, with the centre roofed over to form a large room. There was the sea in front and a rookery in the elms behind. All day, from early morning, the rooks cawed and the surface of the sea glinted like new, hammered pewter.

My sisters went on a day's excursion with the Brownies into Kent. It was spring and they found not bluebells, for there were no woods, but primroses and, for one of them at least, it was a picture-book dream made reality as bluebells would once have been for me. One summer Freda Hands and I took them to camp for a week-end. The twins now were made to go to Sunday school and hated what one of them described as the atmosphere of "gloom, sin and guilt", although they enjoyed the annual Sunday school treat which was held out as bait all the year round. Most of their energies on these Sunday afternoons were devoted to upsetting the Sunday school teacher, who wore a weed-green beret and believed literally in the story of Adam and Eve, which my sisters did not.

On Sunday evenings, in the summer, the family went to listen to the band on the common. I hardly ever went with them because I had more serious things to do, but I used to watch them setting off with my brother carrying a deck-chair for my mother to sit on, for we would not have dreamt of paying for the hire of one. My sisters carried raincoats, even in a heat-wave. They used them to sit on because of the damp that would otherwise "strike up".

I do not know what happened about my father's job as a window-cleaner's assistant. Probably, in some way, it was unsatisfactory, for he soon got another job as the keeper of a lock on the north side of the Thames, near to Chelsea Bridge. There he spent his days, opening and closing the lock gate, waiting for the tide. Sometimes he caught a conger. They were enormous things and, when they were landed, thrashed about on the edge of the lock and barked. They looked as though they could bite too, but we never got near enough to let them try. Besides the eels there were hundreds of little silver fishes in the lock water and dozens of rubber balls came bobbing through the gates. There was driftwood too and once, when the tide was out, my father found a revolver in the mud.

There was one job that I held for a number of months, but it was more because of the tolerance of the employers than any increased efficiency on my part. This was in the office of a wholesale bakery. I was a ledger clerk and I learned to count in dozens, not in tens. In order to fit in with hours of baking and the deliveries of the roundsmen, we worked from nine until twelve-thirty, had three hours for lunch and then worked from three-thirty until eight, or whenever the books balanced. These extra hours in the middle of the day were a boon to me. The house was quiet and no one disturbed my writing. But it meant a break with St. Barnabas Church. My only association with it was through the Rangers. I never went to any services, nor even to "parades", the military aspect of which I disliked, and it was too late, by the time I finished work and had had supper, to go to evening meetings. On Saturdays we often worked until well past nine. I cannot think why, but there was a feeling almost of celebration about these Saturday nights in the office. The foreman from the bakery used to come down and surreptitiously give us cakes and large broken lumps of fancy bread in paper bags. There was a "paradise loaf" which had everything in it, including pieces of pineapple. There were quarterns and half-quarterns, batons and coburgs, wholemeal, wheatmeal, white and stoneground and "tins" which were sliced to almost any number.

We sat on high wooden stools at long, sloping desks which faced each other and which were "standing" height. The glass in the tall windows was opaque and we could not see out. All the people in the bakery were older than I. They had nearly all been there since the turn of the century. Head of the office was little Miss Stevens. She was so small that she could hardly climb on to her high office stool. She had a lugubrious stalagmite shape, as though her natural growth upwards had been almost counterbalanced by the downward drip of the stuff that made her. The gentle bloodhound face was grey and purple. All her clothes, down-flowing, were in shades of mauve and grey. She spoke mild cockney in a surprised little voice.

Miss Crone, in her personal appearance, was a modified form of Miss Stevens; she was a little taller and seemed less completely cowed by gravity. She dressed in soft shades of brown and spoke with a marked Scottish accent in a voice like a silver bell. Miss Clinker was about the same age and had had nearly as long associations with the firm. Her shape was that of a toy Mrs. Noah that had been made for a church bazaar out of a deeply-waisted cotton reel. Her grey hair was coiled on top of her head which altogether looked like a cottage loaf that someone had trodden on, so that the resulting folds accidentally took on the look of human features. Besides these three there were two other people in the office who were only about thirty-five. With one of these I became quite friendly. She was dark and tall with a white skin and blue-grey eyes and she had the manner of a somewhat rebellious and certainly mischievous school prefect. It is a look that many long-legged women have who are not elegant.

When I first went to the bakery there was a pretty little woman of indeterminate age working with us in the office. Her name was, I think, Miss Woods. She had large eyes and straight hair of such a dead black that it looked as though it were dyed. One day during one of those silences that occur in desultory conversation, she remarked:

"Bill said to me, in bed, this morning . . ." and then stopped. Miss Stevens stared blankly through the frames of her oval spectacles and Miss Crone peered up over rimless bifocals. The silence was razor-edged. Then Miss Woods stepped determinedly down from her stool and said that we might as well all know that she had been married for over a year. The bakery did not employ married women and any girl marrying from the office had to leave. This was a policy adopted by many firms during the years of unemployment. Little Miss Woods went immediately into the manager's office and confessed. She left at once and the incident provided a topic of scandalised conversation which only the abdication of Edward VIII could supersede.

From the bakery we could get some groceries at wholesale prices: butter, sugar, dried fruit, flour and breadstuffs. Often, on Saturday night I took home paper bags full of bread and cake that the foreman had given me. I judged from the foreman's manner that this was not allowed, but I knew that it would be wasted if I did not take it.

There was an air of domesticity about the offices of the bakery, concerned as it was with the sale of comestibles at times when only housewives were about. We made tea on a gas ring in the corner of the office and washed up in a bowl on the table there. Miss Clinker used to scrutinise the tea-towels and move everything on the shelves about a quarter of an inch. In the morning and afternoon breaks, we ate new rolls thickly spread with butter. There was a faint air of disapproval from the elderly ladies towards me and I was acutely conscious of it. It was not that I ever did anything particularly reprehensible, but they disliked change and anything new, and I, by reason of my few years, was an innovation. I was an example of modern youth and one of those responsible for all the evils of the modern world, including the abdication. The disapproval was tacit, kindly and quite clear. Then, one morning, I came late into the office and saw signs of hysteria on the faces of the three ladies. They were all off their stools. Little Miss Stevens fluttered in one corner of the room, Miss Crone had her back to a wall and Miss Clinker stood with her wide feet planted wide and her face flushed.

I thought at first it must be a mouse, there were enough of them in the bakehouses, but it was something smaller than that —a caterpillar, an ordinary large green "cabbage white", innocently undulating on the floor against the wall. I could not believe that that was all the trouble, until Miss Stevens gave a squeak which, I think, was the nearest she could get to shouting.

Miss Crone shuddered as I picked up the caterpillar. I went to the outer door of the offices and threw the little creature into the road. Miss Stevens was pathetically grateful, Miss Crone sat for a long time with her hands before her face, Miss Clinker said nothing. Later Miss Crone whispered to me what a brave girl I had been and how she would never, never have had so much courage. I nearly blurted out, as I usually did, that I had not been brave at all, that I did not in the least mind caterpillars and often helped my sisters to collect them and worms and snails too, but for once I held my tongue and left my cake in the grass. I felt I had done something to vindicate modern youth.

For a good deal of our shopping we went to the market stalls in the Northcote Road, although my mother kept her eye on the prices in the Falcon Road area too and frequently I saw her stumping purposefully along beside the tram lines. We never took trams or buses when the distance was only a mile or two. My mother started a "drapery club" in which people had "shares" and paid a shilling a week each. If there were twenty people then one of them could spend a pound each week at the store from which the club was run. The organiser had a free share. We bought quite a lot of things in this way; my mother never found it difficult to arrange, for people liked to be helped to buy things they would not otherwise have had the strength of mind to save for.

The Battersea house was much quieter than the café had been but it was not very quiet, for we all had loud voices and were excitable by temperament. My father was getting old and had suffered cruel disillusion during the last twenty years, but I doubt if it was greater than what my brother and I were having to face at the same time, and out of this dissatisfaction our tempers frequently flared up. There was nobody to pour oil on troubled waters; it was usually much more as though somebody were pouring water into smoking fat. One day my mother jumped up and said she was sick of it all and was going to get out of it. She flung on her hat and her coat and the next moment we heard the front door slam behind her. We were horrified. She had gone.

My father said I had better follow her and I was out of the house in a matter of seconds. It was dark, but I could see her running down the road like a terrapin upended. She put a great deal of energy into her running but she did not get along very quickly and I was easily able to keep within a few yards of her without being seen. After a while she slowed down and I followed her out into the Northcote Road. It was late and the shops were closed, the stalls had gone, but, in St. John's Road, all the windows were on display and the lights shone out of them like Christmas.

My mother, now, was dawdling along; her face was flushed

with exertion and her mouth was pressed into a thin line. Sometimes she stopped and stood looking in at a shop window. She went down one side of St. John's Road, looking in all the windows and then walked up the other side, just lingering. I realised with a pang of emotion that she was doing almost exactly what I had done when I had walked round the miscellaneous stores.

Sonia and I often discussed our respective parents and we had always regarded my mother as a typical housewife, rather dull and content to be nothing but what she was. I realised now that this was not the case at all. Before she married she had worked as a cashier. I think she had been happy in this work. The routine clerical world of business, which we despised, was her world, just as the world of literature and the theatre seemed to be mine. She was as much frustrated as I was, but in a different way. To my mother "a living" was everything; to my father and to me it was the life that mattered and the fact that my father, now, had neither much of a living nor much of a life was a lesson I was not prepared to learn; for my mother, the knowledge that if she had been free, she could have made a better job of keeping the family must have been hard indeed.

As soon as I saw that she was going home again I ran on another way and got there before her. I think she never knew that I had followed. She said nothing when she came in but glumly got ready for bed. We heard a lot, in those days, about "frustrated spinsters" but ever after this the word "frustration" did not call to my mind the unmarried, working woman; it made me think of my mother. She did, in the end, get back where she wanted to be, but it needed a war to put her there and, in nineteen thirty-five, we did not seriously think of it.

The bakery changed hands. The man who took it over seemed to think much of himself as an efficiency expert. He reorganised everything. He walked round the bakehouses and the offices, saying: "Drive on! Drive on!"

I found it impossible to concentrate on anything at all, with this kind of goading and I was one of those who were dismissed. I was not sorry, for the atmosphere had changed. Everyone had become irritable and the roundsmen and the bakehouse men kept cursing under their breath.

My mother was so angry at my losing yet another job that it

was useless to try to work at home. I spent all day in the public library, subsisting mostly on cups of coffee, when I could afford them, and subsisting on nothing at all when I could not. I used to get extremely tired during the day and get a new lease of energy in the evening after I had eaten. This energy used to last until the early hours of the morning and I used to sit writing in my room with my invisible pictures and my pomegranate wallpaper until it began to grow light. Traffic used to start again at about four o'clock in the morning and I used to creep out of the house and go for a walk on one or other of the commons. Clapham Common was best, because the sun came up, like a blessing, beyond the South Side, and it shone through the trees and made a ground-mist of the dew.

Years ago, in what now seemed a different life, I had talked about writing and acting to the Watertons and Alice had said that if, when I was fifteen, I still wanted to act, then I might go to Sadler's Wells to see if I could train. Life had been full of possibilities then, which now seemed hopelessly remote. Sonia had left the Watertons, during the time that she and I had been estranged. Alice had been too much concerned about Sonia who, more than anything, liked freedom, so she went back to Hendon, where nobody noticed much what she did, and I did not see Alice Waterton again, although I knew Donald later.

I had heard of a drama course at Morley College at Westminster and I went there. It was conducted at week-ends, taking up all of Saturday and Sunday. As a course for people who worked during the week, it was quite strenuous, and a number of people went to additional classes on weekday evenings as well. I was surprised to find how earnest each one was. None of them had any doubt that they would become professional actors and actresses and numbers of them talked of "my career" as though they were already on the way to international fame. About this, I think I was the least sanguine of any, but I worked and I continued to write. I did hear of two of these people again. Somebody told me of one who had got a job in a small repertory company and another of them I saw in a minor part in a play that was hooted from the gallery of a London theatre. Perhaps all the other aspirants changed their names.

# CHAPTER X

# TAKE YOUR PLACE IN THE QUEUE

WE were upstairs people now. In the garden that belonged to the people downstairs flowers bloomed and a lawn flourished. My sisters grew grass in a flower-pot for the cat to eat.

I had managed to save enough to buy a typewriter from a little shop in Webbs Road. The typewriter cost two pounds five shillings and would probably have been worth that, as scrap metal, for it weighed about a ton. Even the keys were so heavy that I had to stand it on a pillow, when I typed, in order to deaden the noise, which was similar to that of a pneumatic drill in low gear. I had learnt to type on a teleprinter and my speed on "Big Oliver" must have averaged ten words a minute.

One of the things my brother and I did with our very young earnings was to buy a wireless. Many years ago, in Arundel Square, I sat wearing ear-phones and listening to faint music that "came over" on a crystal set that my father had made. We must have been very young then, because my brother could not remember it. I rather doubt if he was old enough to be allowed to wear the head-phones. Since then there had been no wireless. We were the only people I knew who did not have one. The popular tunes, which everybody hummed, we picked up from other children, but we never really got to know them, and many of the comic catch phrases, which were familiar to them, were strange to us. We were the uninitiate.

First getting the wireless was almost better than when we first had electric light. Our home had background music just like everybody else's. It was perhaps the only pleasure which my brother and I had shared since the days, in Ellington Street, when we let down ropes out of the lavatory window.

For me this satisfaction was shortlived. Previously there had been no music, but there had been the sound of our own voices. Now there was both. The place sounded like a fairground. It did not occur to anyone to look up an attractive programme and then to make a point of listening to it. One merely turned knobs until one found "music". If this changed to "talking", one turned the knobs again. The object was to keep up a continuous flow of unobtrusive tunes.

During the times when I was working, people were always asking me if I liked it and I always said: No, I hated it. They seemed put out when I said this and, obviously, it was not the way to reply, but it did not seem possible to say anything else. Then they asked me what I did want to do and I said that I wanted either to write or to act. Some of them said that everyone went through a phase of being stage-struck; everybody at some time or another thought they could write. When people saw that I took no notice of this they laughed and they did so in just the way that I had laughed at Margery Denotkin over Ernie and the Secret Service. They laughed as though they knew that, in a moment, I would see how absurd it was and would laugh too.

The woman with whom I had become friendly, at the bakery, lived in Sabine Road and I used to go to visit her sometimes. The district south of Lavender Hill was "better class" than where she lived and she was looking for other rooms. She found them in Leathwaite Road which adjoined Shelgate Road. She said that there was more accommodation than she needed and asked me if I wanted a room. I had been longing to make a home of my own and to lead my own life ever since I had left school. The room was unfurnished and I rushed madly from shop to shop, trying, in one week, to get together enough furniture to live with. My mother helped. I had been talking about living alone for the last two years, and now that I was actually going my parents seemed to accept it.

The house in Leathwaite Road was only round the corner and I carried my typewriter there, before anything else. It was so heavy that I had to rest it on a coping, once, to relieve the ache in my arms. My new bed did not arrive on time, and I slept on the floor until it came. Sitting alone in my new room with none but my own possessions around me, none but my own new standards to rely on and wholly separate, at last, from the subtle nuances of class distinction I had known all my life, I felt that I had, that day, flown out of the orbit of the world. Soon drastic changes of staff were made at the bakery; my friend left and found a new job and new lodgings in Kent. After that I was alone.

In Shelgate Road my sisters now occupied what had been my room. Children are good at staring at wallpaper, perhaps because they go to bed while it is still light. Yet, so carefully placed were my little pictures, that they never remarked on them and I do not think they ever knew they were there. In Leathwaite Road the wallpaper was the colour of a slightly brown eggshell and as clean and as bare. The drama school at Morley College took up too much of my time now and I did not continue to go there after the first year. Whenever I had any money I invited numbers of friends home, in a way that I had not been able to do before. I had ceased to attend Girl Guide meetings but people I had met there came to coffee in the evenings. Sonia came to stay and, in the various jobs I had, people I met sometimes came home with me. My friendships were almost as eclectic as my taste in literature and none of my various groups of acquaintances were able to remain in each other's company for long.

I felt lost with no amateur theatrical activities at all and so joined an evening class at the Battersea Polytechnic. The teacher there had a look like Irving in a lowering mood and stamped his foot in the Irving tradition before making an entrance any-where, on stage or off. My work here was not very promising for, although in interpretation I seemed to excel, my voice was too thin for anything I did to be very impressive, but I went, because I enjoyed sharing literary interests and watching the development of stage technique in others.

Wherever I went I was nearly always late. I could not really accept the idea that one might need more than fifteen minutes to get from one place to another. I could not help wondering on those occasions when I was fighting a losing battle with time or space—or was it both? or were they one?—whether the Jewish philosophers and scientists, born at the end of the previous century, might not have suffered from a similar disability which gave rise to their speculations; Einstein, Samuel Alexander, Freud, all had theories of space-time that seemed, somehow, to vitiate the unwelcome truth that the hour had struck and one was simply late.

To be late when one was part of a stage performance was utterly inexcusable. We were putting on a show composed of short extracts from various plays and poems and, in spite of my feeble voice, I was due to perform in one of these. When I left Leathwaite Road that evening I was not exactly late, but I could be on time only by running every inch of the way and I dared not wait for a bus. I had always been able to run fairly well and the small amount of training to which I had submitted on the track had improved my speed. Particularly when I was excited, I enjoyed the sensation of running and went, now, down Leathwaite Road, across Battersea Rise, Lavender Gardens, Lavender Hill, the Latchmere Road and Battersea Park Road. It was all down-hill but it was quite a long way, long enough for me to be able to forget about space-time and, so to speak, to "sit back" on my reflexes and enjoy the sensations of running which had been familiar too long ago. I could feel my head like a negative weight, stretching my spine, lungs like a balloon on a stick and the strong cumulative thrust of my legs as I sank nearer to the ground with the lengthening of my stride.

I would be on time, just. I knew better than to run at full speed right to my destination, so that I should have to stop suddenly, but I was still breathing very deeply when I went on to the stage. And suddenly a great voice rang out, right to the back of the hall, a deep, strong voice with tremendous power behind it. The voice was speaking my lines. It was my voice.

When I came off, everyone was smiling. It was, apparently, something that frequently happened that one suddenly "found one's voice". People had hardly noticed me before, but, tonight, one of the most talented members of the cast was waiting to take me home.

As we walked along Battersea Park Road he suddenly caught me by the arm and said: "Shall we bus?"

With my head still full of Elizabethan drama I was not sure what he meant, but we caught the bus and argued over the fare. He asked if I thought I would be selling my soul for a penny, but I made him take it, because I was out of a job at the time and that penny was so nearly my last.

We sat in a cheap little café on St. John's Hill. It was a café very like the one my parents had had, in Edmonton, but now I was on the other side of the counter. Edmond went walking every holiday. One heard a good deal about "hikers" in the thirties. They were usually caricatured, wearing very short shorts and with enormous rucksacks. It was part of the fashionable influence from Germany, which included a somewhat qualified admiration for the Hitlerian régime and for the psychology of Jung.

When everybody else had left the café we went too. My room at the back of the house in Leathwaite Road overlooked the common and, from where we sat on a seat near some bushes, I could see that little dark window, throwing back the moon-blue gleam from the street lamp. As we waited on the shrouded common, from the distant roads, the little lights, like jewels and like fire-flies, made a bright zone around us. Three weeks later Edmond bought a car.

From the day I left Shelgate Road I was independent. It was a blow to my mother's pride that I should have gone, but I think that, otherwise, she was rather relieved. She offered to let me sleep there until my bed arrived, but I refused as I declined to go back there for Sunday dinners. To have done so would have been to admit tacitly that I could not do equally well for myself. I did nevertheless visit there most week-ends, for my sisters, now, were beginning to think seriously about their scholarships and I, being the one person in the family who had succeeded in winning one, had automatically undertaken to coach the twins. No amount of family ill-feeling could stand in the way of this. The educational future of the children was far too important for personal disagreements, within the family, to be allowed to affect it. And although I remembered, with distaste, having myself been coached almost to the limit of endurance, yet I did not question that it was the right thing to do by my sisters. "The scholarship" was like the eye of the needle. It was the straight gate and, for us, there was no other way.

Sonia and Michael were married in a swift and practical fashion and, for a time lived in Camden Town, in two rooms, one of which was in the basement and the other under the roof. For a short time they were extremely poor in an energetic, lighthearted, Bohemian way, but Sonia was not really happy without quite a few of the amenities of life, so Michael found a remunerative job in an industrial area and sometimes I went to stay with them. Sonia also came to London to stay with me. She loved the city, hated living outside it and she had had to leave just when it seemed that London was beginning to open its heart to us.

One evening Sonia arrived suddenly at Leathwaite Road. Absence made little difference to our relationship; it never would. As soon as we met we continued to talk, in the old way, almost as though we had not left off. It was when we were well launched in conversation that my doorbell rang again. An entire company of Rangers stood on the doorstep. It was no use my trying to pretend not to be surprised. I was. I had invited them for coffee weeks ago and, with Sonia's arrival, had forgotten. Owing to the growth of my other interests I had really begun to forget them completely. All the same they came up and I collected together all the drinking vessels that I owned and prepared to spend the evening with a gaggle of girls, most of whom had passed the age when maidenhood is an asset, and with Sonia. The Rangers were all very nice young women and Sonia and I were both going through an experimental phase, although as far as appearance went my experiments were usually more subdued than hers. Sonia was very small so that she could use brilliant colours and did. There were two spots of orange rouge on her cheeks in contrast to the purple lipstick on her wide mouth, and her eyelids were heavy with emerald shadow under two thin arcs of graphite masquerading as eyebrows. It was not a boring evening, for Sonia and I were always high-spirited in an incongruous situation and the Rangers always enjoyed themselves most conscientiously, but I think it was the end of my association with St. Barnabas or any other church, and when I went walking with Edmond I forgot how my love for the country had partly been acquired.

Our first long walk was in North Wales. I had never before been so far away from London and I had never imagined such country. When the Welsh hills first came into view I could not take my eyes off them. A fortnight was too short a time. I wanted years. I knew it was naïve to feel like this, but I could not help it. I could have spent all the holiday gazing at just one aspect of one mountain, in every change of weather.

The disadvantage of these activities was that one so often returned to civilisation on a formal Sunday evening, dirty, unkempt and scantily dressed. It was worse if one had forgotten one's key and returned to an empty house.

In the house next door there lived a wonderful old lady. She was as thin and straight as the exquisitely rolled umbrella that she carried so gracefully. She went to church every Sunday in a long dress of smoke-mauve silk, a cumulus hat and grey gloves. As I sat on my rucksack in my diminutive shorts and thick shoes that were wet and heavy as barges, I saw her returning from church, holding high her imperious head and marking the crisp beat of her footsteps with light taps of her imperious umbrella.

When she reached me, she stopped. I looked at her uncom-municatively. I had an antipathy towards lavender silk and soft grey kid and I did not admire wonderful old ladies. Her appearance made mine seem more disreputable than ever. She asked if I had spent the day in the country and I said: "Yes." When I stood up I was above the level at which she could com-fortably address me, so I had to come down the steps. She asked me if I had forgotten my key and I said "Yes" again, laconically. Then she said that I looked extremely tired and I must come in with her and have some tea, until the other people in the house came home. I needed a bath, not tea, but the invitation was a command and I humped my pack on to my coarse yellow sweater and clumped up the stairs after her. I had an impulse to take off my shoes before treading on the carpet and only the knowledge that my wet socks would be no improvement on them prevented me. There was a gospel of Buddha on one of Miss Brain's bookshelves and I felt relieved. Most of the dirt that I was transferring from myself to her carpet was cow-dung and this is quite clean stuff really; it is so clean that it is recom-mended for spreading over the floors and walls of the dwellings to which some Buddhists retire for meditation. If Miss Brain had read the gospel, she would know this and might not mind so much about her carpet.

I sat on the edge of a Sheraton chair with a leaf-thin cup and saucer on the table beside me. The little table had a pie-crust edge and I surreptitiously felt the under side of it, almost sure that it was genuine. Miss Brain said:

"This is a very nice chair, Angela," and patted the one beside her. I said I was quite all right where I was and realised, too late, that she had seen the way I felt her table and wanted, merely, that I should admire the chair as well.

On the walls were some original oil paintings which I found attractive and, suddenly, I forgot that I was not wearing a skirt and I put down my cup and saucer and stood before one of them. It was the picture of a small Welsh lake and I had spent twelve hours in scorching sunshine just looking at it and how the dark Cambrian slate frowned down over the placid water. Miss Brain said: "I see you like my paintings."

I had friends who were art students and who painted pictures, but these were much better. Miss Brain said she had had to give up painting because her eyesight failed. In her later work the edges of things were blurred. She said she had studied under Ruskin and wasn't it strange that in her young days students had been much exercised over the question as to whether it was immodest or not to paint a young lady in gymnastic costume and now, nobody bothered about that at all. She told me something of her past life and once said: "Now you can judge how old I am."

I was amazed when I thought about it; she must have been over eighty. She said that she wished she could still paint, because I had beautiful legs. I had been told this before, but not by a lady of eighty who had studied under Ruskin. She said there was a golden glow about me as I stood by the window in the mellow evening sunlight. She made me feel like a figure out of a Titian. I was sorry to leave and went there several times afterwards. She was a wonderful old lady.

Many young people at this time went to the Café Royal in Regent Street to sit at the marble-topped tables and talk, in stage voices, for hours each evening. We formed one of those groups that tend to clot together in popular cafés in evenings and at week-ends. It was Edmond who first took me there. Sometimes we went to the home of one or other of this group of friends and listened to gramophone records, or sang folk songs, mostly in German, which I did not know, although I learnt the words of the songs with their meaning. Some of us, like me, were very poor, living at bare subsistence level. Some were sufficiently affluent to fly to Germany at week-ends. German students joined us, sometimes, and we looked at pictures of children in Hitler's schools, playing pipes and singing. Hitler was doing a great deal for Germany. The Jewish question did not arise.

Freud was considered out of date, now, and everybody talked of Jung. I assumed that he must be an advance on Freud, since he came later, and his earliest work was compatible with Freudian theory anyway. Somebody got hold of Jung's essay on Wotan published in an American magazine. It touched on the "deification" of Hitler. In the later translation (nineteen forty-five) an exclamation mark punctuated this sentence. In nineteen thirty-six there was no exclamation mark and the sentence was the more significant.

My time in the public library, now, was spent in studying Jung. I loved literature, as nearly all of us did, and Jung's symbols and his classification into archetypes I found intriguing. It was over the analysis of dreams that I felt dissatisfied, for his symbolism was the wholly conscious kind of allegory that is used deliberately in nearly all our literature and language. I began to feel that, in spite of his claims, he missed the depths. As an aid to literary technique his work had value; as scientific analysis of the unconscious, none at all. In the interpretation of dreams Jung had nothing more than Joseph, son of Jacob.

This last remark I made, once, during a lull in the evening's vociferation. It earned a laugh. Some seemed to be quietly impressed, but I refused to enter into private discussion when they spoke to me in the foyer later, because I knew that my own ideas were only half-formed and I adopted an amused and casual attitude which I did not feel. What I had fully realised was that amongst these young people one conformed only in non-conformity. The important thing was to find new ways of not conforming. Most of us "drank" but did not smoke, "because smoking was the more pernicious habit". I cannot remember which one of us started that fashion. Those of us who were desperately poor used what little money we ever got to give parties in rooms that had no hard furniture whatever. Some of us were, by the standards of those days, quite wealthy. If any amongst us had only moderate incomes they concealed the fact. Some deliberately went on the dole for half the year while they followed vocations as writers, painters, composers, or while they were studying for external degrees. I found this shocking. I lived in much the same way, going in and out of jobs, which I despised, and writing during the "rest" periods but I would not go on the dole. I had lived on it for too long in my childhood and I could not dissociate it from the means test.

Towards the end of one of these periods of writing I found myself financially in very low water indeed. It was not always possible to calculate the time needed to find a job and, when I eventually did so, it was one that had the dignity of being accompanied by a monthly salary. I needed to work three weeks before I received any remuneration at all.

It was autumn and cold sometimes. The gulls came up the river and out to the common. One could see them wheeling above the trees. Pattering on feet nimble as fingers, a cat came along, after the fish I was carrying. That herring had cost me all of twopence. Prosperity had come and it was no longer possible to buy two pennyworth of pot-herbs and a pennyworth of bones. They would sell turnips and carrots and onions only by the pound and you got bones when you bought meat.

I had practically no food in the house, a spoonful of sweet chutney and some rice, nothing more. Some of the grains in the rice were black. Mice! I was too hungry to mind very much, but I put my fish on the window-sill outside, and sat down to examine the rice, grain by grain. If one was forced to live up-stairs, then it seemed to me good to be very high up. There was a mackerel sky and the gulls, harbingers of inclement weather, flashed light and dark signals against its moodiness. Grey back against grey cloud. No gull. A turn like the flick of a wrist and a bird was shining white and patting the sky with soothing cloud-tipped wings. There was the soft curved throat and feet like small hands tired and curled on a white pillow. There was the tender, dove-like breast, the slaty wings, the crimson eye, the yellow, predatory beak.

I sprang up too late. The gull had got my fish. He had lulled me with images of gentle bosoms, fern-frond hands and then had stolen my supper. Sagging in his flight, he went over the roof-tops until he dropped his burden on to the houses somewhere in Muncaster Road. I ate the rice, when I had cleaned it and cooked it. I ate the chutney too. All that hungry night I thought of the fish and how, when the cats and the gulls had finished with it, the phosphorescent bones would gleam, in the dark, like moonlight, broken by wind-crazed water, herring-boned.

The next day I travelled by Underground in the rush and crush of the London morning before nine. Very gently like a gas light when the pressure fails everything faded, sight and sound and all. Change at Charing Cross! The crowd bulged out of the train like paste from a tube that has burst its sides. Everything came back as I passed the sliding doors. Wedged upright, I went with the crowd.

Before I reached Westminster, this tendency of things to withdraw beyond the range of my sensory awareness became too alarming. I had got out of the second train and was on the station platform at Westminster when they finally faded altogether.

I was alone in a very small hospital room. It was bare and light and one had no responsibilities. A young, dark-haired doctor came in and sat down companionably on a chair beside the bed. He was interested to know why I had fainted and carefully and thoroughly he went through all my symptoms, about which I was quite prepared to be communicative. But the old distrust of authoritative power, fear of the workhouse and the dread of having one's own life taken out of one's hands made me determined not to say that I was practically starving.

The authority that had been powerful enough to send our father away, to make him temporarily forsake his home and his children or else see them starve, might well be empowered to effect one's own incarceration in whatever institution existed for people whose own inefficiency and obstinacy had caused them to reach a similar state of deprivation. (Alternatively there were vouchers for food which one could give to a grocer instead of money. These things existed even as late as nineteen forty-five. And it was pointed out to the recipient of them that tradesmen would know of the plight they were in financially, if the vouchers were put to use. When rationing was still in force, people could not even go to a strange shop.) Poverty was culpable; illness was not. And one could never know just what word or phrase would set the official machinery in motion. One false word and one might find oneself in a world of humiliating forced baths at someone else's hands, with evil-smelling soap, a world of floor-scrubbing, table-scrubbing, standing when spoken to and God knows what. There is more than one way of dying for freedom. It was better to keep silent.

I had a blister on my heel and the young doctor wondered if that were infected. It was not. He asked me if I was worried about anything. I said I had the usual financial worries and we both laughed. He asked if I could be pregnant. I said I was not anemophilous. Then he asked if I felt hungry. But half the ordinary feeling of hunger is a desire for oral satisfaction, and this longing goes as hunger becomes real. I was long past the stage when I consciously wanted food. Nevertheless I had eaten a good deal before I left the hospital, although I think they never did discover what curious malaise affected me.

A few days later, one of the Café Royal fraternity told me of a man who was editing a new magazine and wanted somebody to type for him. This seemed more attractive than any job I had heard of so far, and I said I was interested. I was given his phone number, and when I rang him up he invited me to meet him in the café one evening. Both the editor and the magazine are now defunct, but I still have his description of himself in an old diary; tall, thin, greying, fawn suit, flashy tie; but the tie was not so vivid as to dispel the general impression of greyness given by a thin pale face and smooth, fair hair the colour of dried pampas grass.

I saw him in the foyer and he greeted me, at once, by name, so my own description of myself must have been adequate. He coiled his long body into one of the chairs and looked as though he could quite easily have fitted into a large whelk shell. In spite of the turn that the conversation took, there was something ephemeral about him, a kind of cellophane silveriness. He was passionately interested in Spain and later went there, fighting for the "Left". The German folk songs notwithstanding, my sympathies were "left" too, and as I looked up at the gallery where I had sat with Sonia and Michael Campbell and his left-wing companions, I got a ridiculous picture of half my acquaintances walking the town at night, carrying pots of white paint and brushes with which to paint on walls: "Mosley will win!" while the other half went round after them changing the last word to "swing". But the work of the second group was rather quickly scrubbed out, by the police, before it could dry, while that of the first group, oddly enough, remained.

The editor began asking me if I had read certain books, modern works that I had only just heard of. There were disadvantages in being very young. At one point I said that I avoided reading the works of authors whose outlook was as subjective as my own. The editor said that if one merely wrote without reading the work of other people then writing became a kind of masturbation. I said that reading the works of writers who were one's own kind was then like homosexuality and I tried to read the writings of people with an objective outlook and a narrative style.

He said: "You know about masturbation, then?"

I said I had invented it. He asked if I had read Swinburne. Everybody in the Café Royal groups read verse and it was I who, making yet another bid for originality, first said that I avoided it, because I was interested in prose rhythms and reading verse spoilt my ear for prose. I used to say it in a bored, casual way that defied discussion, not because I felt this way about it, but because I did not want my hypotheses made invalid before I had tested them for myself. As I said it now, I affected a slightly superior tone and looked away from him as though I knew that we would both take it for granted that my "ear" was something to be cultivated and cherished but that, of course, I did not talk about it.

The effect of this was just what I had wanted. The editor looked impressed, though slightly mystified. He quoted some Swinburne, which he had probably intended to do anyway, but I said that the rhythms I meant had nothing to do with ictus. The editor looked more mystified than ever and quoted another verse that was no less carnal. I said again that I did not mean ictus. The editor seemed to capitulate and began to talk about the job.

He asked me if I could spell. He said he felt that if we were to work together, one of us should be able to and he could not. I said that, on the whole I could, especially more difficult words, because I became interested in their derivation. I said that if he was sure about double letters, then we might be all right together, because I was weak on those. He laughed and said that was what he called not being able to spell and he did not know about double letters either, since his spelling was Elizabethan.

I wished then that I had lied. It would have been at least a week before he found out and he would have had to give me a week's notice. That would have meant a fortnight of comparative affluence and I needed it badly.

I began to tell him about the seagull and my herring and noticed that his laugh, though high-pitched, was pleasant in tone. It seemed to rebound off the marble-topped tables. But nobody turned round. Nobody ever did in the Café Royal. I told him about my fainting and how they did not know, at the hospital, what was the matter with me. He said it was one of the most beautifully ironical stories he had heard. He said starvation was probably not included in the curriculum in medical schools. He said I should write a story about it and I did, but there was too much prosperity by that time. My story was "out of the mood" and I could not sell it.

Before we met he had asked to see the first few chapters of a novel I had begun to write and I should have known that his own spelling must indeed have been bad if, after this, he needed to ask about mine. I asked him what he thought of my book. He said it was good but that the style was too "rich" and nobody would want to read a whole novel written with the poetic intensity that one associated with verse. Then we were back again talking of literature and literary style.

This editor and I sat opposite each other for quite a long time, drinking coffee. I was very thin and hollow-eyed, now, and I stared at him, wondering if my response to the Swinburne could possibly have been different and willing him to suggest some kind of congenial work or something. He did offer something. He said suddenly: "I'll tell you what—have you ever thought of going on the dole?"

A short time ago I would have been dismayed, but I had learnt a good deal in the last few months. He told me how to set about it and I listened without saying anything. He observed that it would, at least, pay the rent. I was delighted at his suggestion and I knew that my face showed it, because of the answering smile in his. I was delighted because he spoke as though he thought the idea of applying for dole was something quite new and strange, adventurous and rather daring, like going to Moscow or Spain, and he spoke as though he took it for granted that I would regard it in that way too. So I answered in my nicest voice that it was an awfully good idea and I thought, as I stood in the queue at the Labour Exchange, of the gipsy at the door in Ellington Street, and what a long way I had come since then.

# THE DIARY OF HELENA MORLEY
## Translated and Introduced by Elizabeth Bishop

This is the true diary of a young girl, half-Brazilian, half-English, who lived in a provincial diamond-mining town called Diamantina at the end of the nineteenth century. She was twelve when she began it, fifteen when it ends, and through the sharp eye of this high-spirited, gifted child we enter another world. Though the scenes and events of *The Diary of Helena Morley* happened long ago, what it says, as with all works of art, is fresh, sad, funny, and eternally true.

'For anyone reading this Virago reissue, the obvious comparison is with Gabriel García Márquez's *One Hundred Years of Solitude* (1967) . . . What makes it so fascinating is precisely the fact that it represents, as it were, the opposite process of Márquez's magical synthesis.' – Hilary Spurling, *The Times Literary Supplement*